D1545715

It's
NOW or
NEVER...

DEE K. CARTER

CLU, ChFC, RFC

It's
NOW or
NEVER...

HOW TO ENJOY YOUR
LIFE AND NOT LET YOUR
INVESTMENTS OWN YOU

ADVISORS' ACADEMY
PRESS

IT"S NOW OR NEVER:
How To Enjoy Your Life And Not Let Your Investments Own You

Published by
ADVISOR'S ACADEMY PRESS
Pompano Beach, Florida

ISBN 978-0-9975441-6-9

FIRST EDITION

Book and Jacket Design by Neuwirth & Associates
Cover Photography by Jeff Schartz

Manufactured in the United States

10 9 8 7 6 5 4 3 2 1

DEDICATION

For many years, I have considered writing a book, but I didn't know how to get started. Then I met Michelle O'Halloran, the head of Marketing for The Advisors' Academy. She came to me and urged me to do so, saying she was sure I had a book in me. She gave me the final inspiration to get started on this project.

Thanks, Michelle!

In addition, I appreciate all of the work done by Thomas O'Halloran and a very special thanks to Dan Gainor, without whom this book would have never seen the light of day!

There are others that I need to thank. First, my mentors over the years: my coaches, Bob Heasley, David Scranton, and my professors at Abilene Christian University.

But most of all, my parents and my family. My wife Susan has inspired me to be the best I can be and my children, Randa, Devyn, Erin and Mandee, have all, in their own special way, helped make me the best Dad and person that I can be.

There are so many others that I need to thank, but I know I would leave someone out if I tried to write them all down. So, "Thanks to all of you." This book is dedicated to you and all of those people who have touched my life and made it so full!

Dee K. Carter

CONTENTS

Growing Up In West Texas

I WROTE THIS BOOK NOT just to tell stories. My friends and family know I can do that at the drop of a hat. I want this book to help others see some things in my life that might help them learn how to put it all together—all the important things in life. That means faith, family, fun, community and country all in one happy package.

Doing that takes work. It takes faith and it takes the wherewithal to do it all. Commitment, hard work and, ultimately, money. I've heard people say that money makes the world go 'round. They couldn't be more wrong. God makes the world go 'round. Don't get your priorities out of place.

But money is an essential part of that mix. It can give you the ability to send your children to a nice school or put a roof over their heads. It can provide for you when you can no longer provide for yourself. I've run my own financial advice office for 42 years. Ultimately, this book is also about how you need to take control of your financial life.

The way to start doing all that is to take stock of your whole life. That's what I did for this book. It's more than just a trip down Memory Lane. It's intended to be a guidebook, like one you might pick up in a foreign country or a city you've never visited before.

The first section tells a bit about my background so you understand where I'm coming from—in my case, West Texas. Texans know our home is special. As the band Little Texas says, "God Blessed Texas." I've been in enough of the rest of the country to know he blessed those places, too.

Each one of them is special. Each has its own stories and its own character. Texans come from a state with more traditional values and those values make us strong. This section gives you a peak into how they formed who I am.

1.

A Song For Dad

WE ALL WANT OUR fathers to be heroes. I think that's just human nature. To those of us who are children of what people like to call "The Greatest Generation," we never have any doubts.

There's knowing and there's seeing the proof. Through God's grace, I got to see it and it was one of the strangest moments of my life.

The incident reminded me that, no matter how old we get, we never stop living for our fathers. We never stop trying to deserve their legacy, never stop trying to make them proud.

It's an important standard that I want to pass on. I think we've lost some of it and it's essential to find it again.

I was born before the war. America has fought many since—Korea, Vietnam, Iraq and Afghanistan. But to older folks like myself, the war means World War II.

I'm seventy-six and the first clear memory I have was when I was three years old. It was early in 1944 and my Dad was going off to war in Europe. He knew he would be missing father time, holidays and birthdays. Maybe he'd never return at all. He wanted to do something for me—something special. So he got me a puppy.

We didn't have much money at the time, few luxuries. It was a pretty amazing gift. It was a little red Cocker Spaniel that we named "Troubles," *and he lived up to that name.* That dog grew and was part of the family until I was in the sixth grade.

I was too young to understand my father was going off to war or what it meant, probably didn't notice the tears as my parents parted. Military families have endured that for thousands of years and it doesn't get easier.

Dad was twenty-eight years old at the time—just plain old for someone going in the military for the first time. But it was 1944 before D-Day and all the adults knew that the big invasion of Europe was going to happen sooner or later. He wasn't in an important defense industry and that made him draftable. Dad entered the Army and they sent him immediately to Atlanta, Georgia, for officer training. He was smart and had been around. I guess the Army figured that set him apart from the young men fresh out of high school. He was the oldest guy in Officers Candidate School, by far. Naturally, they started calling him "Pops." I still have his annual from OCS[1] and there's a picture of him there with a caption saying "Pops" was the last one up in the morning, but the first one to breakfast each day.

OCS was quick. It had to be. America was gearing up for the big push—D-Day and the days that followed. All the way to Berlin. Dad graduated and became a second lieutenant. Before he knew it, he was shipping out to England.

Dad went on to serve with distinction—as many did in that time. Like most, he didn't talk about it much. A few years ago, I found the medals—two of the blue Combat Infantry Badges. That meant he had been under fire twice—at least. The military people I've met are always proud of that medal. It means they've seen life at its roughest and come out on the other side.

Dad's time in the Army didn't end with the war. He was an ordinance officer and assigned to Germany to pick up the ordinance left behind by the German army, as well as dealing with unexploded bombs. I read a little while back in the Smithsonian magazine more about how impossible that task really was. "Between 1940 and 1945, U.S. and British air forces dropped 2.7 million tons of bombs on Europe, half of that amount on Germany."

It was a dangerous job. Probably why he never talked much about it. The Army transferred him up to Nordenham[2], Germany, and he was there when the war was over.

Nordenham is in the northern part of Germany, just southwest of Denmark and sits next to Bremerhaven. Bremerhaven is the port for Bremen and the name literally means Bremen harbor. The distance between Bremen and Bremerhaven is roughly forty miles—tiny by my Texas standards. That area was going to be my Dad's home for a year after the war. And our family's, as well.

The allies had bombed Bremerhaven back to the Stone Age. Between the RAF and American bombers, they had hit the port more than two dozen times. The allies were putting it back together and already had the shipping channels open.

Mom and my little brother Larry and I took a ship to Germany to live with my Dad in Nordenham. It was a little unusual, but he was an officer and was treated well. We didn't have it bad. We lived in the mayor's home because the mayor had been a Nazi doctor. When the allies took over, he was moved out and we moved in.

My memories are sketchy. Mostly I remember the house we stayed at and that there were soldiers everywhere. Men in Army green. It was like being on an Army base initially. We couldn't bring Troubles with us to Germany, so Dad replaced him with a German Shepherd pup that we named "Harris." I still don't know why we chose such a strange name for that dog.

All this came flashing back to me a few years ago when my wife Susan and I decided to take a trip to Europe. I wanted to see what had become of Nordenham in the decades since the war. I wanted to be closer to my father somehow, to relive what he had experienced.

I don't know what I expected. I guess I figured we'd do a brief tour, see the sites and I'd recall some more about growing up. Pretty basic stuff.

It wasn't anything like that.

Nordenham had changed a ton, of course. It's still quaint. With lots of Tudor buildings everywhere. The town itself is all modernized. You'd never know there had been a war there.

The people were amazing. They treated us like royalty. I've never been treated so well. We spent the day sightseeing the places that I remembered, the different spots where my Dad had worked. We went to the house we had lived in. It's still there, but now it's a house for wayward youth.

They let me go through the building and memories flooded back to me. It's all changed on the inside except the kitchen and the bathroom. It's hard to change kitchens easily. The bathroom was easily recognizable. When I was a child, I had a quick reminder how hot that radiator could be when I backed into it by accident.

The next day, a doctor, whose father had actually known my father, took us around and showed us the place my Dad worked. I learned more about my Dad's time in the Army that day that I had learned living in Nordenham.

It was a sign of things to come.

The Allies converted the hospital into a place for the German soldiers to stay. Thousands were fleeing the Russians and coming north to get to Denmark. These weren't the hardcore Nazis. These were young boys fifteen or sixteen, scared and helpless.

Dad took pity on them and would let them stay at the hospital. He would clean them up and get them out of their uniforms and send them on their way. It was an act of mercy that still resonated more than sixty years later.

It was almost as if my father's ghost was talking to me, telling me things he had never talked about.

I didn't know a lot about my father's war-time experiences. The men who came back from the war didn't talk about it much to their families. They had seen too much, done too much. Then they locked it away to spare those they loved.

I did know he had been to Hitler's Eagle's Nest. He had sent us some photos. But by then the war was over, so they had an almost-touristy feel to them.

The very name Eagle's Nest sounds ominous. It was built by Hitler's personal secretary Martin Bormann as a gift to Hitler on his 50th birthday. The building is 6,000 feet in the air on a rock outcropping in the beautiful Bavarian Alps, near the infamous town of Berchtesgaden, where the Nazi ruler would vacation.

The historian in me wanted to see it, but the son in me found it more important. I carried the photographs my father had sent us that he took when he was there in 1945. I wanted to see if things looked the same. I wanted to envision my father there.

We took the train to Obersalzberg[(3)] and, from there, a bus for the two-hour ride to the top. The ride was gorgeous, with outstanding views of the mountains as the bus went higher and higher up the narrow, winding road.

There's something disturbing about seeing relics of what the Nazis had built. They are simultaneously impressive and terrifying. It's a harsh reminder of what my father and millions of other men and women faced ending the Nazi menace.

Tours enter through a castle-like stone archway and enormous tunnel into the mountain. We felt the temperature drop as we walked into the mountain and climbed on board the impressive, brass elevator. It whooshed us four hundred feet in the air. History books claim Hitler didn't trust the elevator and never liked heights. Join nearly four dozen other people on that elevator and you might see why.

The building atop was surprisingly Spartan, with a large Italian marble fireplace dominating the room. It was a gift from Mussolini, a creepy reminder of what had been. We finished the tour and spent an hour there, but I wasn't really able to connect the photos I had with what has now become a beer garden and restaurant. (*Viva capitalism*).

We headed back down and I was disappointed. I felt I had missed the connection that I was sure was there. That left only the souvenir shop, so I could buy a book about the site. We always buy books when we travel—a nice memento of some of the places we've seen.

The choices in English were pretty limited. I found one with a picture taken looking down into the clouds below. I bought it and headed back to the bus.

I started leafing through the nearly fifty pages of photos as the bus headed down the mountain for the long trip back to Obersalzberg. Then something stopped me, froze me where I sat. I had flipped to a page that showed five GIs sitting at a conference table after the war.

The photo corresponded to one of the ones I had in my pocket. Mine was a black-and-white, grainy picture of the room. This one was full-color and it showed a lot more than just the conference room. It showed five victorious soldiers.

One of the five men was my father.

Dad had died thirty years before, but here I was staring at a photo of him nearly seventy years before. He was a young man again, victorious and proud, sitting in Hitler's stronghold with his friends, including his first sergeant. Together they had survived. Perhaps that was relief I saw on their faces.

I closed the book and opened it again—and then a third time, to get the full impact of what I was seeing. I showed the photo to my wife Susan and she said she recognized Dad right away. I think she noticed the way his legs were positioned.

What insane, unbelievable luck. I went to put a real-life image to the grainy black-and-whites I had. Instead, I get a full-color image of my own father.

It was all I could do not to shout it to the bus. I got up and started showing it around to the other tourists. I don't know how many times I told the story, but it felt eerie every time. Like Dad wanted me to find it.

The tour guide promised to get me two more books for my brothers. Meanwhile, I had photographed the image on my phone and texted to my brother. I just told him this was from Germany when he was three years old. I didn't say anything else. About two minutes later I get this response and my brother was freaking out.

It had been more than seventy years since we had seen Dad that young. Somehow you never forget.

That wasn't my father's only war. Many of the men who survived World War II were thrown back into the hell of combat only a few years later. From fighting fascism to fighting communism. The enemies didn't seem too different to me then and still don't.

Both wanted to control our lives. And my Dad and millions like them stood in their way.

My father was in the reserves and he was recalled to go to Korea, where he fought for two hard years. That was an awful stalemate of a war. The Chinese came in massive waves and tried to overwhelm the allied troops.

I remember when he came home, he joked that he didn't thaw out for six years. He referred to it as his life in the coldest place on earth. He was an ordinance commander and I was old enough to understand better what was going on. We figured, or maybe just hoped, that he had it fairly easy.

Much later, we learned he had been awarded the blue Combat Infantry Badge or CIB which meant he had been under fire. Dad was pretty close-lipped about it all. He didn't want to worry my mother, so he didn't tell her about going on patrol or getting shot at.

That's no different from today's soldiers. The veterans I've met never wanted to worry their families needlessly. They carried the burden. They wanted their families, their children to have better lives.

Whether they're soldiers, or police officers, oilmen or fashion models, all our parents want the same thing for their children. They all want us to have better lives than they did. They want to pass along what they've learned so the next generation has it easier. And pass along what they've earned for the same reason.

It's not out of conceit that they know better. It's out of love to save their children the pain they endured learning their way in the world.

I've lived on God's good earth for seventy-six years and I've been very lucky. Sure, I've made my share of mistakes. Who hasn't? But I've learned and earned and I want to pass along that knowledge.

I've played music and sang with famous people like Roger Miller and competed on a national stage as an Elvis impersonator (and did pretty well, too). I've been a minister and learned that family and community are both essential to a complete life because you fill the world around you with love.

And, I've learned how not just to make money, but help myself and others keep it. Making money is easy, especially in West Texas. It's a mix of hard work, hours and brains. You don't have to be smart to make a lot, but it's what the Army would call a force multiplier.

The problem is that keeping money is a lot harder than earning it. Put it in the stock market and maybe your money goes up twenty percent by the end of the year. Or maybe 2008-2009 comes around and you lose half of it. Taxes take another big hit. And, of course, people spend it too fast.

I've been managing other people's money for forty-six years. It's an important piece of how people can become happy. It's sure as heck not the only part, but when you can't put food on the table or have a roof over your head, everything else takes a back seat.

Mostly, I want to pass along the way to live a good life, a complete life, with the resources to do it right—filled with family, faith and fun.

DEE'S DIRECTIVES:

Make A Budget And Set Goals.

This book isn't just about me. It's intended to be about you, to help you. So after every chapter, I'm going to share just a bit of financial wisdom to try to help you get on the right financial path. The path has a lot of twists in it and I'm not trying to show you everything. This is a start.

The first, best bit of advice I have is to create a budget. This is the most basic and essential thing you can do to take control of your financial life. Too many of us spend without knowing where our money goes. Then, at the end of the month, we are left with nothing. The way to do that is to get a little notebook and write down everything you spend for a month. (If you live your life on your phone, there are a ton of apps that can do this as well.) I mean every candy bar you buy out of a machine, every toll you pay.

Everything.

Use that to start a budget. Figure out how much you spend on average—include money for gifts, entertainment and charity. Then keep tracking your expenses and see how they line up.

If you go out to lunch every day, figure out the average of what you spend including the tip. There are an average of 22 business days every month, not counting holidays. So budget for 22. If you average $10 at lunch, that lunch budget is now $220 every month. Project that out over the year and you are spending $2,640 just to eat your lunch.

Maybe you ought to brown bag it if you can.

The same goes for you coffee addicts. Coffee at Starbucks is a great treat. Dropping $4 for a latte is fine if you can afford it. Buy one every single work day and you're spending $20 a week or $1,040 per year. I bet that office coffee pot is looking nicer right now.

Once you know your budget works, you can figure out how to spend less. That's why you have to track everything. If you pay with a credit or debit card, that will track it for you. If you pay cash, keep the same amount in your wallet every day. At the end of the day, you'll be reminded that you spent money when you notice its light a little money.

This whole art of tracking your money encourages you to save. Because the more you focus on money, the less you spend it. The idea works with counting calories as well.

Now that you've got a budget, let's put it to proper use. Maybe you found new categories you hadn't included. Add them in to keep a more accurate tally. Along with all of your categories of spending, be sure to include a section for saving. Notice I said a section, not one line item.

Here, I want you to list your pension, 401(k) or 403(b) if your employer provides one; an IRA and an emergency account. The first two have tax consequences and are smart moves if you have a stable financial situation. The third is just a must.

Next, budget some of the excess each month into those categories. Try to make each at least $100. If you can afford it, make it more. Over time, stop thinking of that as a number and make it a percentage. Start low but get it to at least 10 to 15 percent. As for the emergency money, we'll get to that.

2.

A Small Town
Country Man

MY FAMILY GOES WAY back in Texas history. I'm fifth generation here and mighty proud of it—dating all the way to 1846, right after Texas became a state. My ancestors were from two of the sixteen founding families of Denton, Texas, just northwest of Dallas. They were the Carters and the Prices, so my Dad was Dee Price Carter. Granddad married a Price and that middle name honored the folks who came out here and settled when there wasn't much out here except land and Indians.

My family arrived in Texas in covered wagons just like something you'd see in the movies or history books. The settlers were farmers and ranchers who went out to the frontier to make a better life for themselves and their children. They went west, like Horace Greeley later urged, because there was a lot of land to be had for free where they could homestead.

You just had to work all day, every day—even holidays. You had to sweat in the summer and freeze in the winter and pray that the weather, the varmints (two-and four-legged ones) and illness didn't break you. Do all that, and with God's help and a ton of luck, you might build something.

Both my parents are Texans—or Texicans[4] as some still say. Mom was from Turkey, Texas, up in the panhandle and Dad came from Denton. We've traced that heritage back to Georgia, Tennessee and, eventually, to the Virginia colony in the mid-1700s. My ancestor John Carter brought his family from England. We're proud of that heritage and where we came from. Prouder still of West Texas, where I've lived most of my life.

Texans are very independent. We love our country without exception. But if something horrific happened and we were on our own, we could carve out a republic and start over. A person who is a Texan is a Texan first and always. Texas is a state of mind.

Growing up in West Texas during the war is almost impossible for people living today to imagine. There are days even I have a hard time, and I lived it.

Life used to be darn difficult for almost everyone. But the people knew it and accepted it. It was the end of the Great Depression and no one took anything for granted. People didn't have the luxuries they have now. Forget the cellphones and other conveniences that make up your day-to-day life, even for many poor people. It was the basic things. Many families didn't have a car and if you had one that was it. You didn't see two or three or more cars per family.

No one had TV. It was still experimental. And even having a radio wasn't guaranteed. The homes were small, not the big McMansions of today. And several generations lived in them at the same time. There were no prepared foods. Cooking required a ton of skill to make and bake from scratch. And time. Go make something from scratch and you'll see what I mean.

Air conditioning? That was part of the post-war boom. You had fans. And you got to sweat. (No one simply perspires in 100-degree, West Texas summers.)

I was born right at the beginning of summer, 1941, in Abilene, Texas, my parents' first child. They had moved there about two weeks before my Mom gave birth. That must have been awful for her, moving when she was more than eight months pregnant. She was tough. She had to be. Both the men and women of that generation were made of strong stuff.

Dad was a mechanic and Mom stayed at home to raise the children as women did in those days. With the Depression, my Dad was lucky just to have a job. A lot of people didn't have work and many farmers lost their land, too. My parents probably hoped they were about to build a new life in a new home.

Only the world had other plans.

The war in Europe had already been going on for close to two years. Franklin D. Roosevelt[5] had called on Americans to prepare for an "unlimited national emergency." The German and Italian consulates were closing down.

I imagine the war clouds over Europe were visible even in a small town in Texas.

The three of us lived in an ordinary house in Abilene, just the eastern edge of what Texans think of as West Texas. It's hot and arid and what rain we do get, washes off because the ground is baked by the sun.

We lived there until Uncle Sam called for my Dad, though I don't recall much of it. He got his draft notice in 1944. When that happened, my Mom, my brother and I moved in with family in Big Spring, Texas, not far from where I live today in Midland.

We moved in with my grandparents while Dad was away in WWII until we joined him in Germany after the war. There were three families jammed in that tiny house. Granddad was employed by the city water department and my grandmother worked for a dress store.

They weren't the only ones working. Mom might have stayed at home, but she still kept darn busy. She and my aunt took in washing to help pay the bills. I can remember the old wringer washing machine system in the kitchen and the piles of other people's clothes. I was too young to recall the rest.

My growing up really began when we came back from Germany. The trip back to the United States was an adventure. It took seventeen days on board a ship before we arrived in New York harbor. My parents treated it like it was a special occasion and it was. Mom was decked out in her fur coat and Dad was wearing his dress uniform. Even my brother and I were outfitted in replica uniforms just like my father, complete with 1st lieutenant bars. You just can't imagine the feeling of pride we had in those uniforms—just like real soldiers.

We headed back to Texas and moved to Stanton, where Dad took a job as a car salesman with the Wheeler Motor Company. That job helped teach him the business skills he needed later. He learned well from some smart folks because the company is still in business today. It's run by the grandson of the man my Dad worked for. That says a lot about their customer service and life in West Texas, too.

Stanton was just a few miles up the road from Big Spring. Its only real claims to fame were the fact that it was built around a main road that ran right through the town and a sign.

The sign was typical Texas. It read: "Stanton, Texas, Home of 2,000 Friendly People and a Few Old Soreheads!" Not much has changed in Stanton except the population. It's still a mighty friendly town.

We lived in Stanton until war came again. This time I was older and I knew more of what was going on. Dad was in the reserves and called back to active duty. They shipped him off to fight in the Korean War for two more years. It was too difficult for all of us to live on our own and we moved back near family in Big Spring.

We found a place just down the street from my Mom's parents, George and Lily Montgomery. George was awesome. He was a serious-minded man with a keen sense of humor. A classic Texan.

George taught me responsibility and how to tell the truth—the old-fashioned way. He had a razor strap hanging on the back of the bathroom door to keep his straight razor sharp and his grandson honest. I'd watch him sometimes sharpen his razor. He didn't need to use it on me… much.

I guess we're not supposed to think like that now. Family used to push responsibility on their children a lot more than they do now. Parents baby their children into adulthood now. We were expected to grow up and grow up fast. The world was a harsher place and adults expected or demanded we stay in line.

One day in sixth grade, I was playing an afternoon basketball game and there's nobody there. Everyone was still at work. And I looked up in the stands and there was my Dad standing in his dress uniform. I hadn't seen him in two years. I remember running off the court during the game actually and running up and jumping in my Dad's arms. I still think of it when I see videos of soldiers returning to their families.

We were thrilled when Dad returned. It was February, 1952, and I'm sure my Mom was relieved. She feared he might later return to the Army. Historians might call it the "forgotten war" now. It wasn't then. It was very terrifying even if it was halfway around the world.

The war wasn't over but thankfully Dad's time in the Army finally was. Our family moved east—all the way to Denton, Texas, my father's home town and the place the Carters originally settled more than hundred years before.

We didn't stay too long. Dad must have longed to be back in West Texas and I sure know that feeling. We lived in Denton until December, 1953, until right after my youngest brother, Robert was born.

Then Dad went into business for himself. He must have saved up a lot of his Army pay because he became the proud owner of the Buick Dealership in Monahans,[6] Texas. That's just west of Midland-Odessa and close to Pecos. Yes, the Pecos from the movies. Though the expression, west of the Pecos means the river, not the town. I spent most of my life just east of the Pecos.

West Texas was almost barren in 1954. Oil had been discovered decades before, so there was a sea of wooden derricks in the land around the town. Monahans was small. Heck, it still is. But the four-lane highway stopped just six miles west of town, so having a car dealership there still made sense. I spent the last years of junior high school in that peaceful town and all of my high school years.

Monahans put the word small in small town and I loved it because everyone was so nice. Older folks might understand when I say it was like a Texas version of Mayberry. Nobody locked their doors. Everything was safe, a great place for children to grow up.

Mom had an army whistle to summon us home. That meant we could go out and play anywhere within hearing distance. Life in West Texas was a bubble—peaceful and family oriented.

That was the year I turned thirteen. My life revolved around school, athletics, family and work. Dad insisted on that last one. He expected a lot from people, especially his own family. And work was always part of his agenda.

That combination worked great for me. School was good, though small like the town. I was a good student, but not a great one, trying to figure who I wanted to be. Somehow I ended up in the honor society; though I'm convinced they just had to fill out the photo. Our graduation class was just eighty-nine students. Shockingly, forty were still alive for our 50th class reunion.

Sports were big and I was a typical teen who enjoyed them a lot. I preferred football, but coach insisted you had to play basketball, too. Sports helped bring me closer to my Dad and helped him teach me some important lessons. Heck, he even got me into radio.

Dad only missed one athletic event I was in for three years. He was sick one night and couldn't show up, but that left us with a problem. Dad was a radio sponsor and, as a former high school player himself, he did color commentary. He was good too because he knew the game so well.

The night he didn't make it, I had to stop by and talk on air. Now, I'm on the radio all the time. Who knew where that would go?

But sports are good makers of men and both my coach and my father proved it. My high school basketball coach was Bill Villines, one of the fairest men I have ever known. He was a mentor, a coach, a friend and a Christian leader who would not allow his fundamental principles to be harmed by what was going on around him.

That wasn't always easy. One time, we showed up at a restaurant after a game. This was before desegregation, only we had an African-American young man on our team. The restaurant said they wouldn't seat any "colored" people in the dining room. Coach Villines told us he thought it was wrong and asked the team how we felt about the situation. We agreed totally. We were a team. We played together, we ate together and, that time, we went somewhere else together.

It was a good lesson. Coach Villines lives in Oklahoma and even now we occasionally visit on the phone.

My Dad hammered home a different lesson. I came home after having a great basketball game and I was so full of myself I was floating on air the next morning at breakfast. I had scored twenty-some points and I was convinced I was the eighth wonder of the world.

Dad didn't put up with that for long. He challenged me to a game of Horse. I must have been seventeen at this point so Dad was hardly what you'd call old and he kept in great shape working. He took the ball first and stood about twenty feet from the basket and did a two-handed shot off the backboard and into the net.

I told him I didn't shoot that way and he just smiled. "Son," he said, "you have to shoot exactly the same shot." I tried but no dice. To make a long story short, he beat me so bad I was embarrassed. Except that wasn't what he wanted. What he wanted was the lesson.

Dad taught me something essential to life. He said, "no matter how good *you think you are* there is always someone else better." I never forgot the backyard lesson Dad taught me.

He taught me a lot of lessons, but he tried to let me learn on my own by doing. I started working at age twelve in the family business. The job was to clean up the tools at night and clean and dust the cars. He wasn't teaching me essential skills. He was teaching me maturity and responsibility.

When that job wasn't challenging enough, Dad bought the Humble gas station, as well. It wasn't big and fancy like today's service stations. It featured just two pumps—regular and Ethyl. I was expected to work after school and when I didn't have sports on Saturdays. We'd fix a flat for $2 and pump your gas in the era long before self-serve. In small town Texas, no one ever imagined that I might get robbed.

It taught me self-reliance, as well as an appreciation for cars, since I worked at both the dealership and the station. When I was fourteen, I figured I better get my license. (Like I said before, we grew up faster back then.)

I drove my red 1946 Ford convertible to the DMV, not even thinking there was anything wrong with it. I saw a man in the car next to me as I pulled up. I went in and took the written test and came out only to find he was the one doing the driving test. He was stunned by my audacity to drive up without a license to go and try to get one. The man told me I had better pass or I'd be walking home.

He climbed in on the passenger side and I took off. I knew I was doing well, but he felt he had me when we got to parallel parking. He didn't know I'd been parking my Dad's cars in the showroom for years. At twelve, I could do everything but make those big cars stand up and dance into a space. I glided right into the spot with just a hint of a smile.

I didn't need the license to know I was growing up.

From my earliest memories, I always wanted to make someone proud of me, always wanted to live up to the expectations that Dad shared with me throughout his life. He was a pretty plain-spoken man who wasn't always "politically correct."

That explains a lot about me and who I am. When Dad told me, and I'm paraphrasing a bit, "Son, if you kick crap, you get it on your foot," I knew exactly what he was talking about. It was his earthy way of saying, "Do unto others what you would have them do unto you."

Dad did live by that rule, even if he didn't know it was the Golden Rule. Personally, I always thought of it as "The Carter Corollary."

I watched him live it so many times when he was dealing with the public. Never once did I catch him in a lie, or even stretching the truth. He wouldn't do it even when it might mean that he would lose a deal.

Those lessons didn't just help me personally. I have tried my best to apply them to business as well.

DEE'S DIRECTIVES:

Max Out Your 401(k) Match.

Most employers use 401(k) investments as a perk to keep employees happy. Those have replaced pensions in most cases because pensions had guaranteed payouts. Pensions were hard to fund for companies because they had to plow in money to meet their obligations in down years. They were also disastrous to workers if the company went out of business and designed for an era when people didn't job hop.

You own your 401(k). No one else does. But to encourage you to save, your employer probably sets aside 2 percent or 3 percent matching funds. (I've heard of employers who go as high as 8 percent.) That means, the employer will match every penny you put into your account up to 2 percent or 3 percent of your salary.

Forget what you earn in the market, you earn 100 percent automatically the first year. Only a fool would ignore that. Investors celebrate double-digit returns. This is a triple-digit return. There are rules about vesting—how fast that money officially becomes yours. Some firms allow it instantly and others do it over time. There are limitations. Check with your human resources department to find out how it works.

I don't care if you have to do baby sitting or cut your neighbor's lawn so you can save that much. Do it.

That's not the only new money you can expect from a typical employer. Most companies give raises, even small ones. Even poor employees tend to get cost-of-living raises. That means you start off every year with more money in your paycheck than the year before. That extra is found money. Don't waste it.

Sure, you need the added cash. There are piles of bills to pay and you really want to buy that nice thing you saw at the store or maybe on Amazon. That's all great. Go ahead and boost the economy for a treat. But before you pay anybody else, pay yourself.

You've been getting by on what you made before. So take part of that new money and set it aside to go into savings. If you are earning an extra $100 a month, set aside a third of that to savings. It might not seem like much, but $33 a month is about $400 a year. And that's not one year, that's every year going forward, compounded.

The median household income in the U.S. is $59,039, according to the Census Bureau. Just a 3-percent raise from that is $1,771.51 over the year. That's about $147 a month, so I'm not picking these numbers out of the air.

Save like that every time you get a raise throughout your career and you'll be saving a lot more. Just $400 a year over a 45 year career, adds up to $18,000 without any increase from investing it. One of the big secrets of having a secure future is looking at your finances over time. Small numbers get big fast when you look at how they add up over a year or a decade.

Save and save some more. You'll thank me when you retire.

3.

How Firm A Foundation

I HAD NO IDEA WHAT direction my life would go when I finished high school. I'd bet that's the case for most young men and women coming of age. I wanted to join the military, but still dreamed of going to college. I knew education was the route to a good career. But in my heart, I wanted me to serve my country.

ROTC was the obvious choice to achieve both goals. I couldn't help but choose the Air Force. What teen-aged male doesn't want to fly jets, even now?

My high school grades weren't good enough for a scholarship and my basketball career wasn't exceptional, either. That's the story of a great many high school athletes. It's easy to be a big man on campus when the campus is small. Once you move to a bigger school, it gets much more difficult.

My destination was Texas Tech. Only I wasn't fast enough or tall enough to play basketball there. I tried making the team as a walk-on and failed. They were a great team in a great conference and I didn't make the cut. The jump from high school to college is enormous. Almost as big as the one from college to the pros. I still had to give it what we used to call the old college try.

My first two years were spent doing ROTC[7] and I loved it. The military regimen wasn't that different than sports. But it gave me a feeling that I was giving back to my country and that's exactly what I wanted. I even signed on for the third year—a huge commitment. When you signed that contract you were on the hook for the next two years to Uncle Sam.

I loved it, but it wasn't easy. Veterans know that military life is always a challenge. And then you add in college. There was a mountain of school work as well as ROTC. Life then threw me an added curve. I injured my knee at a particularly difficult time and had to go home. Dad was going through some financial problems and he was thinking of trying to sell the business. I took off for a semester to help him out and work on making my knee serviceable again, as well.

You never know where life is going to take you. Being away from school gave me time to think about what I wanted to do in life without the pressures of school or ROTC. I started to hear a different calling and, while I was home, I decided I didn't want to go back to Texas Tech. I had a new plan—to transfer to Abilene Christian. They even offered me a little scholarship. That was enormously important. At $18 a credit hour, I needed all the help I could get.

The calling was simple. As you can probably guess by the school name, I wanted to become a minister to work with young people. But that meant Bible study and Texas Tech wasn't the right place for it.

Abilene Christian sure was, especially for me.

It was called Abilene Christian College back then or ACC. Now it's a full-fledged university and I proudly call it Abilene Christian University. My years there became the foundation of everything I am today, everything I stand for. Our 1964 yearbook, the "Prickly Pear," highlighted four essential goals to grow the students into men and women: spiritual development, mental development, social development and physical development. The school wanted to turn us into complete grownups body, mind and soul.

Our yearbook actually quoted one of the early laws of the land— the Northwest Ordinance of 1787—to emphasize that point. It read: "Religion, morality, and knowledge, being necessary to good government and the happiness of mankind, schools and the means of education shall forever be encouraged."

All that fit nicely into the school motto at the time: "First things first forever."

Those were the principles that the teachers brought to every class, every day, whether it was in my field of study (Bible and New Testament) or in secular studies—like mathematics or English.

The switch in schools and in callings was more complicated than I realized. There's a lot of difference in life paths from the military to being a youth minister. I was desperately in need of help sorting it out. Remember, I had signed papers to stay in the military for two more years. It was a serious commitment and I've always felt committed to both God and country. But in that order. Now I had to choose.

At the time, you could get a deferment for being in the ministry. I don't know how they handle it now. School officials advised me to talk to Rep. Omar Burleson. He was Democrat because almost all Texas officials were Democrats back then. But there was something special about him—he had also attended Abilene Christian. That made him a bit more inclined to help a student he had never met.

As a Navy veteran himself, Omar understood the challenges I was facing trying to follow my heart. He wrote a letter to the military that got me out of the agreement. It literally took an act of Congress—or at least a congressman—to get me out of that agreement I signed for ROTC. Burleson went on to serve three decades on the Hill, but I'll always remember how he helped me in a very personal way.

I was at Abilene Christian till 1965, though in some ways my heart never left. I know my soul never did. With the exception of my wife and children, Abilene Christian is probably the best thing that ever happened to me. It helped make me a man and I've been grateful ever since.

The Bible (New Testament) was the perfect major for a youth minister. That even included study in both Hebrew and Greek, so we could read old texts in their original form. I still know some of the Greek, though the Hebrew left my brain almost as soon as it went in. I guess you could say the Hebrew is all Greek to me.

A good education starts with great faculty and we had it—starting at the top. I worked for our President Dr. Don Morris during the time I was in graduate school. He was a man of great vision and integrity. I pray that enough of that wore off on me. He and Dr. Neil Lightfoot, my major professor during my graduate studies, both inspired me. Dr. Lightfoot also had the added benefit of being one of the most brilliant men I have ever known.

The rest of the faculty that I dealt with, were equally impressive. Dr. Henry Speck taught in the Bible Department and was later my boss when he became president of Christian College of the Southwest in Dallas. I also worked for the amazing Dr. John Stevens during my graduate studies when he was alumni director and college vice president. Abilene Christian must have agreed with my assessment of his many skills because the school later named him president.

Everywhere I've ever been, I've found coaches to be some of the best people I've met. Wally Bullington, the head football coach and athletic director, was no exception. He joined Abilene Christian after I graduated and spent twenty years as athletic director. We got to know each other teaching a Sunday school class for two years. He is still involved with the university and is one of the truly great Christian men in my life.

There are probably a hundred more faculty and staff I met at Abilene Christian that helped make me who I am. I'll modify a line I saw used in "Kingsman" recently. Educators maketh the man. They certainly helped in my case.

That instruction led to a bachelor's degree in 1964 and a master's degree in New Testament Biblical Criticism the following year. My thesis might sound boring but it was timely stuff—"A Critical Evaluation of the Text Methods of Westcott and Hort In The Light of Recent Discoveries."

We all left school graduation day in 1965, though in some ways I never left. I try each day to put the things that I learned at ACU into practice with my business and have throughout my career. The goal of Abilene Christian is educating for Christian living and that is what I try to practice every day.

It isn't surprising that the basis of what I learned at ACU can be found in Jesus' Sermon on the Mount—specifically, the Beatitudes. Those are the eight special blessings recounted in Matthew. Maybe the most famous is Matthew 5:9: "Blessed are the peacemakers, for they will be called children of God."

The professional pledge that I have hanging on the wall of my office basically says the same thing as the Beatitudes. There are some basic truths in life about how to act. I have tried to live up to both pledges throughout my professional career.

Some of the most interesting learning experiences from college involved my professors, just not always in class. The late Dr. J. D. Thomas taught me an important lessoning in how to listen that I still employ more than fifty years later. Dr. Thomas was a brilliant man and a noted debater of religious issues—essential at a Christian college. The school sent him whenever Abilene Christian received an invitation to a theology debate.

Dr. Thomas was known for inviting a few of "his boys" to tag along to the debate, take notes and later present a paper to the class on the subject. It was an honor to be included. During my first year of grad school, he was challenged by a well-known representative of a denomination that believed in present-day miracles (healing, speaking in tongues, etc.). Dr. Thomas had his Ph.D. from the University of Chicago and was considered an expert in the subject, so, he was eager to accept the invitation. Honestly, I think he enjoyed the challenge.

I was joined by three other grad students who all "volunteered" to accompany him on this adventure. We had about a one hour's drive from Abilene and were due to be on stage at 7:00 p.m. on Wednesday night for the first night of an advertised three-night debate. (Yes, it's hard to image a three-night debate of religious issues in the YouTube era. But it was a big deal.)

When we arrived, the four of us were shuffled off to one side, where we prepared to take copious notes on the proceedings. Dr. Thomas' opponent was ushered on stage with all the pomp afforded a modern day "prophet." When the two men were introduced, Dr. Thomas offered his "worthy opponent" the option of speaking first—to which he eagerly agreed, ignorant of the trap that had just been set.

For the next two full hours we were inundated with "facts" supporting his position. When he finally sat down, Dr. Thomas approached the podium, looked at his wrist watch and quietly said, "The hour is late. May I suggest that we adjourn for the evening and I will address my worthy opponent's statements when we meet tomorrow evening?" There was almost an audible sigh of relief from the crowd.

Of course, when we began our drive back to Abilene, the four of us who were observing, began to discuss the salient points of Dr. Thomas's opponent. He said nothing and just drove us back to our dorm.

Round two was the next evening, like a boxing match where one fighter hadn't even stepped into the ring. We were excited to be able to hear what Dr. Thomas was about to say, fully expecting him to rip into his opponent's statements from the previous night. When the time came, Dr. Thomas stepped to the podium and said, in his most humble and professorial voice, "Since it has been a full day since my worthy opponent presented his case, I think it might be a good idea to invite him back to the podium to give us a brief resume of what he said last evening."

I remember watching Muhammad Ali deploy the rope-a-dope strategy and it was very similar. Dr. Thomas' opponent jumped at the chance to speak again and proceeded to give us a one-hour "brief" restatement of his remarks from the night before. I think I must have been silently praying for it to end.

When he had finished, Dr. Thomas stepped to the podium once more, and, looking at his watch, said, "The hour is late. May I suggest that we adjourn for the evening and I will address my worthy opponent's statements when we meet tomorrow evening?" This time the crowd looked stunned but obliged.

We four grad students were perplexed and wondered why Dr. Thomas has left the stage without so much as making one point. On our drive back to Abilene, we voiced our feelings and began to throw out all sorts of rebuttals to Dr. Thomas' opponent's presentation.

Dr. Thomas chuckled under his breath and said something that I have never forgotten, because I use it whenever I have a client that has used another advisor in the past and is comparing his presentation with one that I might be making.

His explanation was simple yet elegant. "Tomorrow night, I will take the podium and present my points and my opponent will not be able to attack them at all because, I now know all that he knows and all that I know, too!"

The car grew silent as we processed the brilliance of what he had told us. What he was saying, in his most eloquent manner was listen to all that someone has to say before you make any suggestions. I applied it to my work and think of it in terms of clients. But it counts for any job or relationship. You need to listen to the other person, better understand what he or she knows and what that person's concerns are. Then, and only then, you can address them because you will know all that person knows and all that you know, too.

On another occasion, one of my graduate Bible professors, the late Dr. Henry Speck, reminded me to look before I leap. Dr. Speck gave a final exam in a course on the Pentateuch (the first five books of the Old Testament). It was a course that I took because the subject was of great interest to me.

The final exam was simple: Write a synopsis of the book of Leviticus. We had three hours to complete the exam, writing in long hand in one of those old-time blue books, which had been passed out when we entered the room. No one had computers in those days. We made do with pencil and paper.

I worked on my outline and slaved on the material, finishing within a couple of hours. After I handed in the blue book to Dr. Speck, I glanced up at the board. I read the exam question again and my heart froze in my chest.

I had spent two hours writing on the wrong book of the Bible! I had written a wonderful treatise on Deuteronomy, the last book of the Pentateuch. I felt a sinking feeling in the pit of my stomach that went all the way to China. I stood there for what seemed like years thinking about what I had done.

What had happened? Why did I spend two hours writing an answer to the wrong question? I don't even know if Dr. Speck realized I was upset, it all happened so fast. I was perspiring heavily as I started to leave the room. The realization of what I had done was sweeping over me like a tide. An F would cause my grade point to drop sharply and might even cause me to fail the course.

I had to do something. I had to man up. I turned and went back into the classroom and hesitantly asked Dr. Speck if I could speak to him outside. Now he could tell I was upset. I felt so stupid.

He joined me in the hallway, carefully closing the door behind him so not to disturb the rest of the class. I explained my mistake honestly. He turned and went back to his desk to retrieve my blue book and brought it back to the hallway where I stood trying to keep my composure. I don't think that I was succeeding.

He briefly thumbed through the book, reading what I wrote. Then with a little grin, he looked at me and said, "Well, Dee, you chose a really difficult book to summarize. I would have never used that book on a final exam, but you did a really outstanding job. However, you did not answer the question that I asked!"

I think my heart stopped beating. But he continued before I could respond. "Now, what do you know about Leviticus?" I began to babble about all that I knew about Leviticus, how that book contains the original wording of the Ten Commandments. I kept on going, doing my best to recall everything we had covered or I had read on my own.

Finally, Dr. Speck raised a hand and said, "I see that you know both books well. That is to be commended, but I can't give you the A that I think you would have earned if you had read the question correctly. So, I will give you a B, which will keep you from falling from your A status in the class."

Then he summarized the lesson I never forgot. "I want you to remember this: Always read the question carefully and make sure you are answering what has been asked!"

When a potential client comes to my office, I listen to the questions and make doubly sure that I answer the question that is being asked and not answer based on what I think was asked.

These stories show both the benefits of attending a smaller college or university where the professors know their students and take a genuine interest in them. Secondly, I learned that knowing and caring are two very different things.

Dr. Thomas knew his material, but he cared about the feelings of his audience. Dr. Speck understood that everyone is different and if they do not ask the right questions, you need to phrase it for them. But you should always allow your client or boss to ask the questions and you should pay close attention to what that question is. Then go ahead and answer it with the very best of your ability.

Lessons learned from two wonderful teachers.

I stayed active in the Alumni Association after graduation, first as an active member of the Wildcat Club since graduation. (ACU's mascot is the Wildcats.) This is the group that supports the ACU athletic program. Over the years, I have done my best to say thank you to the school, serving on the alumni board for six years. That included a term as alumni association president in 2004 to 2005.

Giving back in an essential part of life. Think of it as paying forward. You don't have to get a return. You ensure that others do. It's a strategy I've tried to follow—even when I didn't have much to give.

That's led to a relationship that spanned more decades than I care to count. The university has found numerous roles for me to fill over the years. I helped out during our centennial year back in 2004 and I even try and help recruit players for whatever sport I'm watching—from football to girls' volleyball. If I see somebody who looks really good, I send the name to the coaches. I go to my granddaughter's volleyball games and can't help but do a little scouting. There's one starter on the volleyball team this year that I helped recruit. I've done the same at my granddaughter's basketball games.

I am currently a member of the ACU Champions Circle—a group heavily involved in the construction of a new football field on the campus. Last year, the president of Abilene Christian, Dr. Phil Schubert, came to see me. He wanted to discuss some ideas for expanding the university's presence in Midland.

Phil walked over and put his arm around me and said they wanted to do something special to thank me for all I've done for the school. He mentioned the total amount that I had given to the university since my graduation and, I'll admit it, I was shocked. I could have bought a new Mercedes Benz with that money.

Only I purchased something far more important—a legacy. The school and its entire good works are part of that legacy. The discussion brought back some fond memories of faculty and staff that are a huge part of making me the person that I am today. The list of names is too long to include here unless I write a sequel.

Phil said, they thought long and hard about how they wanted to thank me and came up with an ideal gift. We've known each other for a long time and he knew I spent twenty-eight years as an official basketball referee—sixteen of those in college from Junior College all the way up to Division I. So they decided to name the Officials' Dressing Room after me. The Texas Sports Officials' Association recognized me as a Lifetime Member in 2003. But this was more thrilling. I'm told there will be a plaque there and I can't wait to see it.

A plaque is incredible. The legacy is more important. It gave me a chance to honor someone who still means a great deal to me.

My first wife's father, Morris Howard, made a lasting impression on my life. So much so, that the scholarship that we established at Abilene Christian University is in memory of Morris and Doris Howard. Morris was the city manager of Monahans and a Christian through and through. His son Bob was my best friend and it was only natural that, when I met Bob's little sister, I fell for her like a ton of bricks.

Morris ran the City based on Christian principles, not on Christian faith. I'm sure there are people who will read that and not understand the difference. He wasn't forcing anyone to believe as he did. He simply lived his faith by how he treated everyone. I never met anyone who worked or worshipped with him that did not think that he was the finest man that they had ever met.

I relied on his counsel and he was the one I turned to when our marriage was on the rocks. Even though it was his daughter that was involved, he really kept me from going over the edge. When Morris passed away, I was humbled to be asked by the family to sing one of his favorite songs at his funeral and say a few words about a man that had helped me shape my life.

We all have centers in our life that we rely on. Outside my family and my faith comes Abilene Christian. The school gave me the knowledge, skills and maturity upon which to build a life. Just like in the Bible, it's my rock. I treasure my time there and am thankful every day that I had the opportunity to attend college at Abilene Christian.

DEE'S DIRECTIVES:

Automate Your Savings Plans.

OK, we've talked about saving. But if I asked you to remember to set aside money every pay period, we both know that you wouldn't. You'd get distracted or, more likely, you'd have things you want or need to pay for.

That way leads to disaster. Learn financial discipline. Treat your savings like a bill. Set it up in your bank or through your job to pay automatically, every single pay period. After a little while, you won't even notice it. You'll just look at the 401(k) or IRA statement and be pleasantly surprised.

Two thirds of Americans don't contribute to a work retirement plan, according to Bloomberg. Some of them don't have the option, but the excuse for many is they just don't do it. They ignore the paperwork when they first join or forget to sign up when they become eligible. You need to be in the other third.

That doesn't mean you shouldn't put more in if you get a gift or a bonus. I'm just saying that you need to do it this way because human beings are easily distracted. We promise ourselves we'll pay in later, if we can spend now. Only we don't. That's how we got a $20 trillion national debt. Living in the now. You need to live for the future, too.

That's one of the areas where financial advisors are used to helping—planned savings and retirement accounts. We are also here to help people manage life events—inheritances, retirement, sending a child to college. We can also help out when bad things happen—a death in the family, a car accident that leaves you unable to work for three months and more.

That old expression about saving for a rainy day is important. We don't get much rain in Texas. But when we do, the ground is packed so hard and baked by the sun that we get floods.

Those kind of disasters happen in everyone's life. You can count on it. But few people are prepared. Sure, you buy life insurance or get it through your employer. But do you have money set aside for when the heat pump blows up or when your car needs $2,000 in repairs? Probably not.

I recommend creating an emergency account and you should automate this, as well. Credit unions are great for these. Make the account in a separate institution than your ordinary bank so you aren't tempted to access the money. And just set aside a little bit each pay. This gets added to your budget as another line item. So the savings section might read:

- ▶ 401(k)/403(b)/Pension
- ▶ IRA
- ▶ Emergency Account
- ▶ Total Savings

I'll leave it to you to put dollar figures after each of those. Stick to the numbers and help them grow over time and you'll have the beginnings of an actual savings plan. You'll be on track for retirement and even prepared for emergencies.

That way, when the rains come, you'll be prepared.

4.

Bless The
Broken Road

THERE'S AN OLD QUOTE that says, "Into each life some rain must fall."[8] I think Longfellow wrote it, though I'm pretty sure I heard it first as a song. To be honest, I've always loved music. So I probably heard a lot of things first as a song. Either way, it's a truism—life rains on our parade eventually.

The thing about storms is you often don't see them coming. I sure didn't. Instead, I was sure I was sunny and bright.

I started dating my high-school sweetheart Anne when she was a freshman and I was junior. Her parents were great folks, or very trusting. They had to be to allow a fourteen-year-old to go out with a sixteen-year-old. That's hardly Jerry Lee Lewis territory but it was edgy in 1957. We dated until I graduated high school in 1959 and went to college.

Texas Tech was two-and-a-half hours from Monahans where Anne lived. I spent a lot of time and gas driving between the two to protect my territory. Neither one of us was happy when her family moved across the state to Irving, Texas, just prior to her senior year. Her Dad left his job as Monahans city manager to take the same position in

Irving, a Dallas suburb. It was a nice upgrade for him, but hard on her and us.

She liked Monahans and had high visibility as a varsity cheerleader—sort of a big fish in a little pond. Irving High School was about ten times bigger and about twice as far away for me. We did our best to make do with the move. I made the five-hour trip to Irving several times that year to see her and her family and we talked on the phone, though not as much as kids do these days.

Distance took a toll and we drifted apart, only to get back together in 1961, when we both enrolled in Abilene Christian. She was coming in as a freshman and I was a second semester sophomore. Our relationship escalated as young love does and we decided to get married in the fall of the following year. We were married on Labor Day, 1963, in her home church in Irving. She was twenty and I was twenty-two.

I started my adult life like I was living out a movie script. I married my high school sweetheart just like some film plot. Only Hollywood always makes *happily ever after* seem easier.

Here I was, not even graduated from college and we were on our way. My wife worked for the university and I was unloading trucks for Morton Foods[9] every afternoon from 1 to 5 p.m. to help pay the bills. My life was school in the morning, work in the afternoon and school work at night. It wasn't easy for either one of us. Somehow we muddled through.

I think I wondered how we managed even then. I'd get up at God-awful thirty every morning and grab a quick breakfast. And usually fill in some last-minute studying, too. Then I was off to class for a few hours. I arranged my class schedule so I had time to work in the afternoons. The world didn't revolve around student loans as it does now. I had to work.

I'd grab a quick bite for lunch and I would drive to Morton's in my 1954 Buick Century, unloading truck after truck. Work time was divided into boxes and crates of every food you can imagine—pickles and chips, vegetables and meats. And frozen foods—heavy and cold to handle much of the year. Even on warm days, I'd be wearing winter clothes to work in the freezer. Then I'd melt as soon as work was done, trudging back into the Texas heat.

Anne would fix dinner and we'd get a little time to ourselves before I'd have to crack the books and study till late at night, usually at the library. It was quiet and I had all the reading materials I needed. Weekends weren't much better because we had to jam in all the chores, along with my school work.

I know we weren't special. A lot of couples have had those challenges or much worse. That doesn't make it seem any easier.

That was our life for a year before I got into graduate school. I really enjoyed the studies, but I've always been that way when I liked a topic. I'd been thinking seriously about doing religious work after college.

Graduation came in a flurry of speeches and thrown mortar boards and it was time to settle down to the business of the real world. Young people today have coined a term called "Adulting."[10] Then we just considered it growing up.

The school work and the master's degree gave me a chance to do what I wanted. I went to work as a Minister of Youth and Education for the 21st and Eisenhower Church of Christ in Odessa, Texas. It was a great place close to where we grew up and I still have some amazing friends from there. That didn't last because I grew antsy. The time flew by and in a little more than two years, I had the opportunity to move to Arlington, Texas, at the Randol Mill Church of Christ.

Randol Mill was closer to my wife's family and that $15 more per week they offered was a big deal. The position even provided a house, which was incredible for a young family. I did that job for about two-and-a-half years before I had an unexpected visitor come to our house late one night.

It was 10 p.m. and I heard a knock on the front door. Nobody came knocking at that time and I nearly tipped over the lamp I was sitting next to in surprise. The face at the door belonged to one of my professors from Abilene Christian[11]—Dr. Henry Speck—and I thought the world of him. He was on a recruiting trip and he was trying to get me to join him at a new Christian junior college in nearby Garland. He asked me to come be the assistant to the president.

He was a man on a mission. The school had to raise $1.7 million in the next two years and he wanted me to be a part of it. I knew it was a great opportunity because I worked with Abilene Christian in my last year in graduate school, fundraising with the parents association. I resigned the church and we were off to Garland where I spent two years as Dr. Speck's assistant. I even taught a class of psychology, because I had twenty-four hours of psych in college, coached the debate team and assisted with the basketball team. I had to check my schedule daily before I went to the campus to see which hat I had to wear!

We made the $1.7 million goal—something to be proud of. Only it wasn't enough. The school announced it was merging with my old alma mater Abilene Christian. As least we were staying among friends. They came out and offered me a position to go back to Abilene Christian. There was a hitch. They also wanted me to get my doctorate. I had other options. Dr. Neil Lightfoot had received his doctorate at Duke in biblical textual criticism. He wanted me to go to Duke so badly that he made arrangements for a teaching assistantship. I turned it down because I was done with school. It was time to get out and see the world.

I really thought that working as a youth minister would be the only thing that I would ever do, but I soon learned that what I thought was a life-time journey would only be a stop on the way to bigger and better things. I had already altered my original path and switched into other areas of ministry. I was ready for a major change and it was going to be bigger than I ever envisioned.

Knowing you want a change is different than knowing what you want to do. So I began to flounder. I didn't have a job and that just wasn't acceptable. I'm still working in my 70s. You can imagine how hard the idea of unemployment was to me in my 20s.

I was open to anything. I had a lot of people skills—some natural and some from working in the ministry. I tried to focus on positions where those would be helpful. I interviewed with a little insurance company in Arlington, Texas, called Trans States Security Life Insurance which I don't think exists any more.

It didn't start out as an easy job. I went to work with them on straight commission with no salary. That meant borrowing against my life insurance in order to get started, because I didn't have the means to go without an income. Mom had taken out a policy on me as a child that had a $2,000 cash value. Then I borrowed against another insurance policy and ran up a humongous debt in order to get into the insurance business.

That sure turned out to be a good move. I became successful almost immediately—one of the leading producers in the company. Within a few months, they promoted me to a manager. In a short time I had rebounded—from being unemployed to managing five or six other guys.

Another promotion soon followed and in two years I was vice president of agencies. I was still young and my rapid rise shows they were a bit starved for talent. I had the whole state of Texas to go out and recruit agents. I'd hit schools from Austin to Wichita Falls.

I was better at recruiting than some of these young men would ever be at selling insurance. A few of the guys who wanted to sell insurance could barely spell it. But they'd still pay the $200 for the class. My heart wasn't in it. I couldn't bear thinking some of them would lose that money. Two hundred bucks was a lot of dough back then and the company just didn't care whether they passed, as long as it got paid.

I was working with my best friend Buck Sorem and he came to me and asked what the heck we were doing. That was it. He offered to help me find a position with New England Mutual of California, where he was from. Buck resigned the following Monday and my boss begged me to stay, saying he couldn't lose his two top employees at the same time. He gave me a great deal for six months.

It was 1973, finally time for me to move to California—living out of state for the first time in my life. My new company was one of the largest insurance firms in LA. It offered to help us find a place to live; only Anne wasn't really interested in leaving Texas. She went, reluctantly.

Then circumstances intervened—awful ones. Once we got to LA, Anne discovered she had a fibroid tumor. She couldn't have the surgery and take care of our daughter Randa. So she moved back to Texas to be with family and I stayed in California to keep my job. It was supposed to be temporary.

Looking back on it now, that seems naive. It was all so emotional at the time, I don't think we realized.

Anne never came back to California after she recovered. My family stayed in Irving and I was still in LA. In a short time we separated. There's no glossing over how that feels. If you've ever been in a failing marriage, you know. If you don't know, count your blessings.

That lasted two years as I drifted, throwing myself into my job. I missed my family and felt broken. Then, in August, 1975, I got the phone call that changed my life forever.

Dad telephoned me one morning at five a.m. Even though it was seven where Dad was in Texas, he knew the time difference. It was too important to wait.

He had received a very bad report on his health from his doctor and he needed me to come back to Texas to help him with his businesses. By this time, Dad had his own automobile agency and was trying to get a Quarter-Horse business off the ground so he could manage that in his retirement.

My initial reaction was based solely on his health. I was ready to drop everything and go home. Family is everything to me. Looking back, Dad wasn't stupid. He knew how lonely I was and how much I missed my wife and daughter, who were living in the Dallas area. This was a nice excuse to get me back to Texas and to give me a chance to get my family back together.

My decision was an easy one. It didn't matter that I had been Agent of the Year at Bill Shelton's New England Mutual agency the previous year. The coveted "corner office" I had earned was just another piece of real estate. Texas had a lot of real estate. Still does.

It's easy to move out of your home when you don't want to stay. I sold all of my furniture, rented a trailer for the small amount I wanted to keep and hit the road within thirty days.

I heard a Pat Green song called "Southbound 35"[12] many years later and it really struck me how similar it was to my experience leaving California. It's about a man heading home to, "let Texas fill my soul." The live version starts off with, "What the hell am I doing down in Kansas City, I know damn well it ain't where I belong." My Daddy would have washed out my mouth with soap if I had said it that way, but that was me in California. Maybe anywhere else but Texas.

The whole way back reality started to hit. I was thirty-four with no job or a place to live and no income. Talk about starting over. I had lost almost everything—first my family and now my job. My career plans had changed and every time it looked like I landed on my feet, it was like they landed on a hot stove and I jumped again.

I was trying to be strong for my Dad and optimistic about reuniting with family. Honestly, though, I was scared.

More than forty years later and I'm still stunned by what transpired. What has taken place since that October in 1975 is truly remarkable. It speaks to the way God leads us in our lives when we are too weak to go on by ourselves.

I arrived back in Texas on a crisp October morning in 1975, after a two day marathon from North Hollywood. The relics of my previous life were all jammed into a six-foot U-Haul trailer. It was hard to be totally depressed. I was back in Texas, after all.

The first thing that I did when I crossed the State Line was to stop at a Whataburger and get a real hamburger. Texans have had the best burgers since 1950 and I was desperate for one. I had been eating at In-N-Out Burger for nearly three years. No matter how much Californians love them; they weren't enough for this son of Texas.

The drive from El Paso to Midland took about five hours and grew more shocking with each mile. I had been living in crowded Southern California and had forgotten how barren West Texas really was. The Texas countryside is one of the wide open spaces people long for, so they have room to live. I felt a sense of relief that I hadn't felt in a long time.

I was home.

It took a while to get settled. My first few weeks were spent living at my Mom and Dad's house and traveling back and forth to the Dallas area to see my wife and daughter. I wasn't ready to discuss it, but I hoped and prayed we could reunite. Things were looking up. They even came to Midland to have Thanksgiving dinner with the family.

I wasn't exactly a great prospect at that point. There I was with no job, no place to live, in my mid-thirty's and back home living with my parents. I was essentially working as a ranch hand for my Dad. He had four mares, one great stallion, an older riding horse that Dad rode and an English pony that had to be the meanest animal I've ever met. He kicked me in the chest around that Thanksgiving and broke two ribs. I don't think I was cut out to be a cowboy.

It was a life betwixt and between. I wasn't in a career job. I wasn't back with my family. I felt lost. At night, I would wander down to a local hotel that had a bar and listen to the young lady named Lynn who was singing there. She was a good pianist and I really enjoyed her voice. She was a good friend of my Dad's secretary and would usually invite me up to sing with her when I came in. It was bittersweet. I enjoyed it, only it made me miss my music even more. It also made me homesick for my family.

Just after Thanksgiving, I went to Dallas to see them. Only I didn't get the answer I wanted. I learned she really had moved on and was even dating another guy. I didn't blame her though it was still a shock. We had been separated for two years. We talked it over and mutually decided to go our separate ways. I filed for divorce soon after that.

This is still one of the most painful events of my life, decades later, I felt lonely and abandoned. I blamed myself. Maybe we just got married too young and grew apart.

I still think highly of Anne. We have remained friends for over 40 years and have grandchildren together. Everything worked out—eventually.

Now, I missed my music more than ever. It has been said that some of the world's greatest songs are written by people with broken hearts. I figured I could fill the Top 40 with hits given how I felt. And even though my songs weren't Motown gold, they still helped me keep it together.

The breakup made me more determined to find a new career. I needed an anchor and my work had filled in when my personal life had faltered. I really didn't want to waste my financial services education. I had earned my Chartered Life Underwriter designation and had passed the Series 6 and 63 examinations, becoming a Registered Representative. I began to look for an opportunity in the Midland area in insurance.

It wasn't enough. I moped the way people do who have broken hearts. I worked and listened to music. And I withdrew. I was in a bad place.

Once more my Dad intervened. In February, he and his partner conspired to introduce a young lady to me. The one they had in mind was a beautiful young woman who worked for Dad's business partner, an oil man in Midland named Ron Britton. Ron and Dad wanted to get me to meet her. They thought that we would make a great couple.

Susan was a dark brunette with blue eyes that just leapt out and slapped you in the face—only you had to notice her first. And, truthfully, the first time I was supposed to do so, I missed her entirely. I was delivering some papers that my Dad said that Ron just *had* to have right away and Dad was "too busy" to drive the three blocks to deliver them. Would I do him a favor and drop them off?

Of course, I did. Only I was so focused on doing the errand that I never even noticed the beautiful, dark-haired girl in the office. Thankfully, she noticed me. She called Dad's secretary to find out who that was that came by Ron's office. The plan had worked—sort of.

A week later, the plotters tried again. I was renting space at my Dad's office, trying to get my insurance operation off of the ground. This time Dad said he had some errands to run and would I mind also watching the used car lot while he was gone? Sure, I said.

Susan showed up ostensibly to look at a used car. This time, I noticed her. WOW!

That was the day Susan walked into my life. I will never forget how struck I was that afternoon. She was so tiny and then I looked into her eyes and it was like she cast a spell on me. We began to date and things in my life started to look up. That was around the middle of February.

I was incredibly taken with her. Here, I thought that I would be a lonely bachelor for the rest of my life and suddenly I couldn't plan a day without her. Just after Susan and I decided to get married, my career really started to take off. I'd argue that Susan was my lucky charm, since I've felt lucky every day since I met her.

Bob Heasley, the general agent for Lincoln National Life in El Paso, was looking for a manager to work in the Midland-Odessa office to assist him in expanding his operation. Susan even went with me for the interview. When we left the meeting, she said, "That is the man that you need to be working for!" I wisely took her advice and on April 15, 1976, I began a twenty-five-year working relationship and friendship with one of the greatest men I have ever known.

What's funny is that Bill Shelton, who mentored me in Los Angeles, had even recommended Bob when I left his agency and moved back to Texas. Only that was a tumultuous time and I never even tried to contact Bob.

He became the second mentor in my business life.

Bob Heasley was my teacher. I might not have wanted to go back to college. I never said I didn't want to learn. Bob taught me how to be a businessman and how to manage an agency. More than that, he taught me self-discipline, a virtue that I find terribly missing in most young people entering the financial service field today. He taught me patience, a virtue that one must possess when starting a fledgling business. And he taught me how to listen, a talent that one *must* have if he or she is to be successful in this business.

Bob was like a sculptor. He took a block of stone and chipped away at my parts and helped me shape my leadership skills like a true artist. He helped make me a better man. He was a friend, a mentor, a teacher and the most caring person that I had ever met in my career.

I had Bob teaching me how to be better at work and Susan bringing out the best in me in the rest of my life. I truly believe God put both of them in my life, even if He did have some help from my Dad with Susan. We were married just a few short weeks after my divorce was final. Susan and I were married by my uncle Charles at his home in Midland. That was June 22, 1976—one of the best days of my life.

It took me a while, but I found the one person that I simply could not live without.

Don't Live Within Your Means, Live Below Them.

This is one of my biggest frustrations as a financial advisor. I've talked about savings and I hope you're converted. Now I'm going to discuss its opposite number—spending. We all have to spend or we can't live. That's not the issue.

I'm talking about the American disease. Overspending.

America isn't the land of milk and honey from the Bible. It's the land of excess and we are bombarded with it. Turn on the TV or go out to a movie and you see actors and actresses decked out with the latest gadgets, driving the hottest new cars, living in huge homes and wearing only the finest designer clothes and jewelry.

Awards shows are fantastic examples. Watch the bling at the Oscars or the Golden Globes. They even have a red carpet so everyone gets to model their high-end fashions and pricey jewelry. Everything is handled by design consultants, hair dressers, makeup people and so on. They employ an entire entourage just for one evening. I know a bunch of Texas millionaires and I can't name one who would ever do this.

It's hard not to want to live like the stars. Only you can't. Unless you have Bill Gates money or are becoming the new J.R. Ewing, you can't afford it. Stop trying to live like you can. Check out paparazzi photos of celebrities on their day off. They don't dress that way. They dress like ordinary people. Even they realize that sophisticated lifestyle is unsustainable 24-7.

I just wish the rest of the public would realize it. We're caught in a quest of what used to be known as "keeping up with the Joneses."

Only these days, it's probably the Kardashians and that's even worse. Just Kim Kardashian and her husband Kanye West are worth an estimated $335 million. They can afford that entourage.

Trying to live like that costs us plenty—on bigger homes, fancier cars and maxed out credit cards. The result is terrifying.

The Federal Reserve Bank of St. Louis reports that the typical American savings rate is a pitiful 2.9 percent. That's total, savings and investment. Back in 1960, it 11.2 percent. That's still a bit low, but much more realistic. And in that era, many people had pensions, too. The savings rate stayed mostly over 10 percent until 1985. It's been that way ever since except for a brief blip that was probably just because of a stock market boost. We save about one fourth of what we use to save.

There's an easy solution. Try to live below your means.

Guarantee you have some excess every month. Go back to your budget sheet. Make sure there's a miscellaneous line and allocate some money to it for extras. There are always expenses we don't account for; things you'd say are random. Make sure you have money to handle them. And if there aren't any that month, shift some of that extra cash into savings.

Either way, try to spend under what you budget when possible. You budgeted lunch out twice a week? Limit yourself to once and bank the extra. The same goes with every single budget line. Try to spend less.

Living Life
To The Fullest

ENJOY YOURSELF.

No, that's not exactly my motto in life. But it's a good suggestion on how to act. My life took me on a lot of twists and turns. I have few complaints. Because I tried to have fun along the way.

Put better: Pursue your passions. Do what you enjoy. One of the things I enjoy most is singing. I've played with a 16-person backup chorus and performed in a nationally recognized chorale. I've packed away probably $20,000 worth of Elvis outfits and paraphernalia in various locations from my time as an Elvis tribute artist. And it's been my pleasure to perform on stage with big names like Roger Miller and Roy Orbison.

I still sing at the drop of a hat. If there's a soundtrack to my life, it's filled with Elvis, Johnny Cash, Roy Orbison and enough gospel music to satisfy Mahalia Jackson and Johnny Cash at the same time. Singing keeps me young. Singing keeps me happy.

Singing also lets me thank God. Psalm 95:1 says: "Come, let us sing for joy to the Lord; let us shout aloud to the Rock of our salvation." If the Bible recommends it, it sounds OK to me.

Part of my enjoying life has been to see things and go places. My passport is filled with stamps all across Europe and the Mediterranean. Seeing the beauty and history of the world is just one more way to enjoy your life.

That's not all life's about, but it's an essential piece of a life well lived.

5.

All I've Got To Do
Is Act Naturally

HOW DO YOU DESCRIBE a life philosophy? My flippant nature makes me want to make jokes, only life is too important for that. So, I'll get serious for a bit.

A few years ago, I remember then-Indiana Governor Mike Pence telling people, "I'm a Christian, a conservative, and a Republican, in that order." While that applies to me, it doesn't define me. It's a series of nouns, not a strategy. Not a philosophy to live by.

I have been told, by experts who study this kind of thing, that your philosophy of life is pretty much formed by the time you reach age six. I can barely imagine that. I was still trying to figure out how to use my Big Chief Tablet and No. 2 pencil at that age. I do know that my parents' attitudes about life and other people have been some of the largest influences in my adult life.

That's one of the many reasons why family is important. Good lessons stick with you. So, unfortunately, do bad ones. Everything good about who I am started with my parents. We were never told that we were better than anyone else. I like to think of that as the Texas way.

Northerners who dislike Texas don't really know us. Take a look at the Cenotaph[13] that sits across from the Alamo. It honors many brave men who fell fighting for Texas independence and sits on the location where their bodies were reportedly buried.

They were a mixed lot. Some had traveled all the way from Europe—Germany, England, Ireland and Scotland. Others represented most of the states in the young nation, from Vermont to Virginia. Many of those who fought and died would be called Hispanic today. Then, they were simply Texicans. Now, they are simply our heroes.

That's the Texas I grew up in. My brothers and I were raised to respect everyone, regardless of race, color or creed. That was hardly common in the era my dad taught it. But it stuck.

Dad carried that through from home into the workplace. He always told me that when you had a choice to make about who to hire for a particular position, you always hired the person that was best qualified for the job. That was regardless of their age, sex, color or religion. It's something that I learned from him early on. And it's something I always applied in my business. My Dad's philosophy helped make him a success.

One day, while I was in high school and working in the parts department of his automobile business, our janitor came in to look at the new Buicks. Willie did the janitorial work for a number of dealerships in Monahans. So he wasn't exactly "our" janitor. He was a contractor, a businessman in his own right.

Willie was a black Texan who always wore a cowboy hat and bib overhauls, pretty typical in the late '50s in West Texas. He would come in, after hours, with his beat-up pickup full of brooms, buckets, mops and pails, and clean the show room. He worked hard and took pride in doing the best job possible. I know Dad respected him a lot because of the work he did.

Willie came in one afternoon while the sun was still out, which was out of character for him, and began looking at several new cars on the showroom floor. None of Dad's three salesmen even came out to talk to Willie. They looked at the clothes, not at the man who clearly appeared interested in car shopping.

After a few minutes, Dad walked out of his office and walked right up to Willie. He didn't focus on the clothes. He just talked to the man and asked if he was thinking of buying a new car. Willie said, "Well, Momma wants a new Buick and I came by to pick one out." Dad showed him the cars and Willie decided that he wanted to buy a new, 1957 Buick Century.

Dad told him what his price would be—more than $3,000 at the time—and asked him how he wanted to pay for it. It was at that point that Willie opened the top pocket of his overhauls and pulled out a roll of bills and started peeling off hundreds. He told Dad with a sheepish grin, "Tell me when I have given you enough."

He paid cash for that car. Dad tried to take it in stride. I think the other salesmen were still picking their jaws up off the floor. Dad filled out the paperwork and Willie said, "I'll bring Momma by after five when she gets off of work at the hospital and pick up the car." The three salesmen watched in stony silence.

After Willie left the showroom, Dad walked over to them to hammer home his point. "Do you guys realize that by ignoring Willie you missed out on a really good sale and a good commission? May I suggest to you that you stop allowing a person's appearance to affect whether or not you serve them. If you can't follow that advice, you won't be working here very long."

It was one of the most effective teaching situations I have ever experienced and it has remained with me for sixty years. To this day, regardless of how a person is dressed, how he or she looks or how that individual may talk, I remember Willie and the lesson I learned that day. It's sure helped my career. Running a business in the oil patch means you meet millionaires with worn jeans and dirt under their fingernails. At the same time, some of those three-piece suit types might not be worth a plugged nickel.

That was one of hundreds of lessons Dad used to teach me about how to treat others.

He always taught me that "whatever is worth doing is worth doing right." Dad didn't just mean work. He meant life. He meant everything you do—from parking your car between the lines to treating your friends and family properly. It's an attitude that used to be common—not just in Texas. The Greatest Generation had it. It helped them win World War II. Then they brought it back with them from Germany and Japan. It was part of how they moved on from all that they had seen and done ending that horrible war.

Dad taught me right from wrong, of course. He also taught me that there are people out there who simply choose to do wrong because they don't love their fellow man. He had to explain to me that there are people who cause chaos and are just out to do as much harm to others as they can. He was right. I've seen it too many times. Now, with the internet, it happens daily. Even victims of tragedy are targets—the families of Sandy Hook, the wounded in the Las Vegas shooting, the victims of the church shooting in Sutherland Springs, Texas. Evil feeds on itself as it seeks to harm the innocent.

And that's why Dad always reminded me not to get too caught up in it. He told us that if we treat such people the way they are treating others, we are only hurting ourselves. His oft-repeated saying, which I will paraphrase because he was a man of plain words, was, "If you kick manure, you only get it on your foot."

That's a fine place to start for deciding how to live your life. Only it's not enough. Most of my life has been influenced by Christian teaching that I learned at church and at Abilene Christian University. The Golden Rule, which is oft-maligned, is still the first thing that I try to think of when dealing with others.

Do unto others as you would have them do unto you, is also close to the professional pledge that I have on my wall from the American College, where I received two of my professional designations—Chartered Life Underwriter (CLU) and Chartered Financial Consultant (ChFC).

It states: "In all my professional relationships, I pledge myself to the following rules of ethical conduct: I shall, in the light of all conditions surrounding those I serve, which I shall make every conscientious effort to ascertain and understand, render that service, which in the same circumstances, I would apply to myself."

This is the goal that I have every time I meet a new client or start a new relationship. It has served me well over the forty-six years that I have been in the financial services business, but it has also served me well in every relationship in that time.

My family life is more harmonious when I stop to remember that I am first to serve and after that to be served. (I'm sure my lovely Susan is reading this with a chuckle. I'm certain she remembers every time I have failed at this.) It is better to give than to receive doesn't mean that one can't receive. In fact, learning to receive from others is something that everyone needs to do.

It is a humbling experience to realize that we are *not* the center of the universe and that we need those around about us to complete a full and beneficial life. My goal has always been to first understand and then to be understood. I can't stress strongly enough that a life that is self-centered is one that will never be able to influence the lives of others or to assist them in their needs.

This all probably sounds corny, but it is a truism that has ruled over my personal life for many years. I won't pretend I have always followed the rule. None of us is perfect and I sure don't pretend to be. There were times when I was younger that I not only felt I was "bullet proof," I was very full of myself. Shocking, I know.

Life has a way of humbling you and beating that out of you. The failure of my first marriage, the birth of a Down Syndrome daughter, the loss of my parents, the near failure of my business in the early years of my career, are only some of the times when life reminded me I'm not perfect. All of those incidents and many more brought me to where I am today and to what I am trying to do today.

My goal is to be the best husband, father, friend, Christian and businessman that I can. I realize that I will fail on every one of those. Each time, I plan to try again—whether I succeed or fail. Using my faith and my philosophy of life, I pray I will be able to reach my goals and succeed in all of these areas.

Not long ago, Susan and I took off and drove to El Paso just to have dinner with my mentor Bob Heasley and his beautiful wife, Mary Lou. That's a four-hour drive, for a two-hour dinner, but I wanted to tell Bob, one more time, how much I appreciated him and what he had done for me and Susan. His words were short and simple, "Thank you! Now, go and do the same thing for someone else!"

That attitude has helped me through some strange times in my life. I've seen some of the more unusual sides of living as I pursued first the music business and then life as a nationally recognized Elvis impersonator. It helped as Susan and I have traveled over much of God's good Earth and learned that people everywhere have goodness in their hearts.

Through it all, I've tried to keep in touch with what's truly important in life. That list is a simple one—family, faith, community and nation. Susan, my children and the rest of those dear to me have kept me going over the years. Combing that love with my faith helped me endure the hardest times.

We're more than just family though. You've already seen how much I love Texas—especially West Texas. And I adore this nation, which has given all of us such opportunities, and the men and women in the military who defend her.

Americans have been given some incredible blessings—first by God and then by our Founders. Few of us can live up to them, but it's important to try. One of the ways I attempt to do my part is by giving back. We all need to do so—in charity, ministry or some other way. I try a mixture of both—helping others either by volunteering or in my financial work.

I don't think of myself as a perfect model. I'm a man—no better or worse than you. And if I can do it, then so can you. It's important to do good. It's also essential to have fun while you're at it. We aren't here forever. Let's all make our mark.

DEE'S DIRECTIVES:

Debt Is Your Enemy.

If the American disease is overspending, then one of the worst symptoms is debt. Debt is simply an obligation to someone. When you tell a friend: "I'm in your debt," you aren't legally obligated to them. When you tell a credit card company the same, you owe them, often with crushing interest.

The statistics about personal debt in our country are as staggering as they are terrifying. The average household owes more than $137,000, according to the Treasury Department.[14]

While you try to process that number, here's where we stand as a nation:

▶ Our household debt now totals $13 trillion, according to Forbes[15]. That's gone up more than 16 percent since 2008, hardly a good trend.

▶ Most of that is in mortgages—$8.7 trillion of it. That's fine unless we have another housing crash, then that number becomes incredibly important.

▶ Another big factor comes from student loans—$1.4 trillion. You've noticed a lot of talk in Washington about wiping that out, which means we all tack that on to the national debt.

Our revolving credit, which is mostly made up of credit card debt, has now hit a record high of $1.042 trillion, according to the Federal Reserve.

It's pretty easy to look at your own finances and decide whether you feel good about your numbers or not. But I want you to do more than that. I want you to calculate your own debt number. And, yes, I know that sounds scary. It won't take long. Add together what you owe—mortgage, student loans, credit cards, personal debt and bills you haven't paid yet. That number was your personal wake-up call. If it's less than the national average, good. If your house is paid for, your student loans wiped out and you pay your credit card off each month, then you are a debt master. Mortgages, of course, can take 30 years (or more sometimes) to pay off. So if you didn't overreach, that debt is understandable.

Student loans can take years to pay down as well, but you'd better have a plan. The rest of the debt is simpler. Try to pay off the credit cards and loans with the highest rates first. Use interest-free transfer deals to stop racking up more credit card debt. Be sure to read the fine print. But the best way to stop paying more on credit cards is to stop using them if you can't pay them off each month.

You heard me right, just stop. I didn't say cut them up. Credit cards are useful and convenient. Don't abuse them. They help you make big purchases without carrying around a ton of cash and they easily allow you to track your expenses. They also make spending too easy. One way to kick this habit is to gradually shift your minor spending to cash. You don't have to carry around a fat wallet to pay for lunch. Then you can keep the cards for major expenses and emergencies. You can better monitor them that way. Debt is like anything else in finance: It's fine if properly managed. Most of us don't manage it. We let our debt manage us. Pay it down and then pay it off.

6.

King Of The Road

LOVE MUSIC. ALWAYS HAVE. I'm one of those people who always has a song in his heart—and often coming out of my mouth. If you've been paying attention, every chapter and even the title of this book reflect my love for music. "It's Now Or Never" is both the perfect title for what I want to say and the advice I want to give, but it hints at both my love for music and The King of Rock 'n' Roll Elvis Presley.

I started singing as a child. I have a letter written to me by my Dad while he was in Germany during WWII encouraging me to learn a song for him. "Your Mother tells me that you are quite a singer!" he wrote. "You will have to sing a song for Daddy when I get home." I don't remember whether I did or not, but I feel like I've been singing all my life. I don't think Dad was disappointed.

Mom told me that I would actually stand in my crib when I was just a baby and sing the songs from the radio at the top of my lungs. That sounds cute now. Boy, I bet I drove her and the neighbors crazy. Picture a baby barely able to talk bellowing out pop songs, off key, as loud as humanly possible. I don't think I give my Mom enough credit.

I guess the music bug stuck. I grew to love music more and more. On my 15th birthday, Mom and Dad gave me a Kay acoustic guitar. It was a thing of beauty—the two-tone wood and a pair of white accent lines running around the edge enhancing it with a touch of class. It was love at first sight. And when I picked it up, it just felt perfect in my hands. If dogs are man's best friend, guitars can't be too far behind.

The first song that I learned to play was "That's All Right (Mama),"[16] a tune that had just come out that month on the Sun Records label by Elvis Presley. I purchased the 45, but to give you a hint of when this was, the song also was released on 78 rpm, as well. I didn't know it at the time, but it was the first of dozens of his songs I would learn and perform.

I went from The King to the Man in Black. Not long after my first song, I picked out "Walk the Line"[17] by Johnny Cash and began jamming with a few of my friends from high school. I was punching above my weight—all of those friends were a couple of years older than me. I had just enough talent to hold my own.

But it was when I started singing that things started to change. I was asked to join a local group that played at the area youth centers in Monahans and Odessa and the small towns in the area. The next thing I know, our little five-piece band was traveling around playing music by Buddy Holly and other country greats.

I played music all through high school and had some nice adventures doing it. I'm sure we loved playing because of the music, but it didn't hurt that the girls liked it, too. By my senior year, I had formed my own band, The Rebels. I know, what teen doesn't want to be a rebel even now? We were getting fairly well-known in West Texas as one of the "rock 'n' roll" bands that could be hired for almost any event. Rock was still young and we were riding the wave of popularity.

Our group was following in the footsteps of another West Texas boy, Roy Orbison, who had a band called the Wink Westerners. They were playing some of the same venues we were playing, singing "Hey, Miss Fannie"[18] and some of Roy's fun early stuff. You always knew them by their signature Roy Rogers bandanas they each wore. Roy's band had one over us. He was also playing on TV every Saturday afternoon on a 30-minute show on KMID-TV [19] sponsored by Pioneer Furniture. It was the big time as far as we were concerned.

We never made it to that level, but we came close enough to play with Roy in person. It was a street dance on July 4, 1959, in Kermit, Texas. That's just about eight miles from Roy's home in Wink, Texas. (I bet you know where he got the band name now.) Fourth of July is important in Texas and though Kermit wasn't a big city, it was still a good-sized gig.

There was Roy right there in the audience. He was one of us, just a good ol' West Texas boy and we all knew him. He came up on stage during a break and asked if he could join in. I think it makes a better story to tell outsiders who don't know how close West Texans really are. There we were sitting on stage next to Roy Orbison and he was like one of the band. He performed with us and even sang his most recent recording, "Ooby Dooby." It was cool to be performing with him. He was one of the greats. It was also the first time I'd be on stage with a national celebrity, though it sure wasn't the last.

I had to put my singing career on hold for a couple of years after graduating high school. Those were the basketball years and playing took a lot of practice time, even though I didn't make the team. Any athlete will tell you game time is short. Practices are long. That all changed when I switched colleges. As in so many other ways, Abilene Christian made all the difference in my life when it comes to music. It really was the place I needed to be.

I auditioned for the Men's Glee Club and was accepted as a second tenor. I said, I had the bug and I meant it. I wanted to entertain people. You might call me a bit of a ham. Only if you've ever seen the audience respond to a song they love, you'd understand. God gives entertainers their skills—the ability to write songs, play instruments or sing. We give it to other people as a way of saying thanks.

I sang with the Men's Quartet and was a part of the group for the two years while I worked toward my degree. I was also part of another small band. I had set aside rock for a while. The Kingston Trio and The Brothers Four were popular on the radio then, so we did mostly folk songs and lighter rock. (I can probably still do a good rendition of "Tom Dooley.")[20] I also sang for a lot of church functions and almost anywhere else I was asked to perform. When you are willing to sing for your supper, you get a lot of invites.

Folk music wasn't just on the radio, it was part of the culture at the time. It was on TV and in movies, more influential than music has ever been because of mass media. "Where Have All The Flowers Gone"[21] by Peter, Paul and Mary was a popular request for our group. The trio traveled around representing the college a little bit and I continued to be part of the glee club. The club was composed of twenty-eight young men with good hearts and strong voices. We were really pretty talented and did tours all around the Southwest. It was a great time.

I kept singing the rest of my time in college—even through graduate school. My first job, after graduation, included serving as the regular song leader for all of the services of the 21st and Eisenhower Church of Christ in Odessa, TX. I played my guitar and sang for nearly every church gathering. Just picture me with a Bible in one hand and a guitar in the other.

It wasn't long after we moved near Dallas before I was singing with a group that entertained all across the Dallas and Fort Worth area. (Airplane passengers know the area as DFW now thanks to the airport.) But I didn't really get back to music until I moved to Los Angeles in 1973. LA was a happening music town in the '70s.

Soon after I hit LA, my wife Anne became sick and our marriage grew strained. I was living alone in a three-bedroom apartment meant for my whole family. Lonely hardly scratches the surface of how I felt at the time. I started driving six blocks down the street for dinner. The place had a great restaurant and I knew the chef since my agency had the group insurance at that restaurant. The chef was a master and I would go there because I was sure to get a great meal.

One night, I ventured into the club area where a four-piece band was entertaining. They were quite entertaining and I was able to lose myself for a while. The evening really lightened my mood. I made arrangements to host a company dinner at the restaurant and club several weeks later. It was bound to impress everybody.

I needed a refuge from my troubles and I turned to music. I began to frequent the restaurant-club, located in the North Hollywood area where I lived. It had a real nice feel and I was always comfortable there.

My best friend, and business partner, Buck, was to be my co-host for the event. We didn't have the internet then to look up the club schedule. So we unfortunately planned the event on the "talent" night at the club. We were enjoying the parade of talent that evening, such as it was, when I heard my name called as the next contestant.

Unbeknownst to me, Buck had entered me in the competition. He thought he'd pull one over on me. I didn't blink an eye. I just walked right up on stage and started singing. It wasn't a contest. It was more like no contest. Due to a real lack of competition, I was awarded first place for the night—a whopping $200. I had a blast. As I recall, the $200 didn't come close to paying the bill for the night.

A couple of nights later, I was at the club having dinner and listening to the music when the leader of the band called my name. He went by Jack Daniels,[22] because he shared a real name with "Dragnet" TV star Jack Webb. I ended up doing a full set with his band Silver Creek and I was a hit.

The club manager liked me so much he hired me to emcee Wednesday talent contests. From that point, I became a regular with the band, usually sitting in with them for the talent contests and on Fridays and Saturday nights, as well. It helped lighten my load and keep me out of trouble.

The club was an exciting place to be. We'd perform on our own or play back-up for some of the then-top country stars. I played along with Silver Creek while they backed up stars like Don Williams, Roger Miller, Merle Haggard and many other "lesser lights" as they paraded across the stage. Merle wasn't too surprising since it was called "Hag's Place" and he was a part owner. Backing up the amazing Emmy Lou Harris[23] was extra special because I got to meet and get to know James Burton and Glen Hardin, two of Elvis' musicians who were playing with her.

Music was the high point for me during those two years. I either performed with or for a lot of stars who dropped into the club from time-to-time. Hag's Place was just a short drive down the street from Universal Studios where such shows as "The Glen Campbell Good

Time Hour" were being shot. So, it wasn't unusual to have guest stars like Mac Davis drop by. We never could get Mac to join us on stage, but he and I had some fun swapping stories about our experiences being raised in West Texas. He was from Lubbock, as everyone recalls from his great song, "Texas In My Rearview Mirror!"[24]

The nights I played with the band, we'd do maybe five sets which is a lot of music. That meant we got to meet a whole bunch of famous performers coming through. Though the club was open, it hadn't even had its official grand opening. They finished the restaurant and Merle showed up for the grand unveiling. He had created an old cowboy country club and for me it was a bit like being back in Texas.

Those years at Hag's Place were a constant peek into the world of celebrity. One night we're playing poker in the back and a pretty gal walks in. She was a little over five-foot tall, with pigtails and wearing Levi's and a white shirt. It was Barbara Mandrell[25] in her early years before she went on to sing, "I Was Country When Country Wasn't Cool." Only a few years after that meeting, she was named the Country Music Association's "Female Vocalist of the Year" two out of three years.

Roger Miller came in one night with Robert Lansing, one of the stars of the TV show "12 O'clock High." Miller was a nice, unassuming guy and he asked to sit in with us. He didn't want to sing, he just wanted to play. Imagine that, performing songs with Roger Miller accompanying you.

It takes ego to sing in public, but it's intimidating to sing a song made famous by someone in the audience. They were all great about it and I found all of them to be very complimentary and willing to offer advice to a weekend singer. I know that flies in the face of some of what we think of celebrities these days, but it was true. Celebrities were able to be themselves more in the days before social media like Facebook and Twitter.

After we were done playing each night, the band would always go down and have steak and eggs or something to 3 a.m. Then we'd wander back to my place and play music or write songs till the sun came up.

It was LA, so naturally I was "discovered" one night by a talent agent, Jay Chevalier, who offered to represent me and get me on the stage in Las Vegas. He was involved in the construction of a new hotel/casino/showroom there and searching for "new" talent.

As much as I loved music, it wasn't the right move. I was surprised at the offer, but knew how difficult the life of an entertainer was from visiting with the many stars that had drifted through Hag's Place. First off, I was too old to start a new career. Singers don't start at thirty-three. It's a young man's or woman's game. I also had a "legitimate" career in the insurance industry and didn't want to take the risk. He was persistent over the next few weeks, but even agents learn that no means no.

Jack Daniels, who went on to play lead guitar and back-up vocalist with the country group Highway 101, was one of the most-memorable guys I used to play with. He's an incredible guitar player and played lead guitar for the band. He was also the one I turned to for help when I had to move back home to Texas. I didn't have the money to get back so I went to Hag's Place and looked for Jack. I asked him if he wanted to purchase my Fender Stratocaster 1959. It was a two-tone beauty with a white pick-up guard and I think it's now worth like $15,000 to $20,000 or so.

Silver Creek later broke up and Jack went to Tennessee to pursue his career. One night many years later, I was watching Country Music Television and I saw something that had me calling for Susan to come and see. There was Jack Daniels on TV with my Fender Stratocaster. Highway 101 had won the CMA "Vocal Group of the Year" and here he is on-stage with my guitar. My guitar made the big time and I was sitting in my living room watching it on TV!

Music was still important to me back in Texas. I was in a club one evening during Karaoke and some guy got up and sang an Elvis song—and he butchered it. One of the people I was with turned to me and said he barely recognized the song and he commented how the singer had thought he was so great. But my friend knew I also performed the same song and he asked me to do it. The other man had left so I reluctantly agreed.

I walk up to the stage and start singing and I knew I was knocking it out of the park. I could see it on the faces of the audience. Only halfway through my performance, the guy walked back in. Here I am singing the same song he did, only much better. I felt guilty but what could I do.

When I finished, the guy walked up to me all angry and said, "You just sang the same song I did." He was steamed but everybody around us just died laughing and he walked away. I think he finally realized he wasn't any good.

Poor Susan heard tons of music stories from my time in LA. She didn't know whether to believe half of what I told her when we first met. Remember, everything's bigger in Texas. Sometimes that includes tall tales.

I got a call one day from Doug Atwell, who was the fantastic fiddle player with Silver Creek, and he invited me to sit in with them out in Albuquerque. It was six hundred miles away, so Susan and I spent the night with my brother in Lubbock and went straight to the club once we hit town.

We arrived in Albuquerque late in the afternoon and went straight to the club where the members of Silver Creek were having dinner with their families. We all ate together and everybody got along great. The band started performing and Jack Daniels said, "You know, we know a guy from Texas who we'd like to have join us." I went right over and got to sing and play with them the whole rest of the night.

I don't think Susan had believed all my LA stories until then. But that made a believer out of her.

Back to Midland, I was still involved in music. I went to a couple of clubs here in town and played with a couple people I knew. Clubs weren't really part of my plan at that point. But I was performing everywhere else.

If there was a company party, I'd be there "a pickin' and a grinning," as they used to say on "Hee Haw."[26] If someone's birthday party needed entertainment, then I'd go for my standards—mostly Elvis and Johnny Cash. I entertained for company dinners, both on a local level and even a National level.

Susan sums it up better than I ever could. She likes to say that if I opened the refrigerator door during those years, and the light came on, I would do fifteen minutes right there. It was at one of those church parties that led me directly back into a new singing career as an Elvis Tribute Artist.

DEE'S DIRECTIVES:

Learn To Zig When Others Zag, As My Friend Dave Scranton Says.

I read everything Dave Scranton writes and I've absorbed a lot of his wisdom. One thing he suggests is going against the grain, learning to zig while everyone else zags. I like it. It appeals to my view about not living your life as a sheep. The crowd isn't always right. The crowd got caught in the dotcom crash and the disaster of 2007-2009 because everyone was afraid to say maybe things weren't right. The crowd follows and that means you get caught when it goes the wrong direction.

Learn to lead. Not just lead others, lead yourself. Sometimes following your gut is a good idea. I don't mean piling your money into

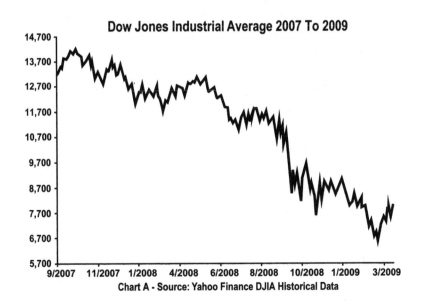

Chart A - Source: Yahoo Finance DJIA Historical Data

lottery tickets because you dreamt the number 5. I mean standing up for yourself. Just because the mob wants to risk their life savings gambling, that doesn't mean you have to do it. Learn to stand out and stand up to the pressure to run your finances like everyone else does. Forget keeping up with the Joneses. Be better than them. Spend less and invest the way you feel is right for you. Not the way CNBC or The Wall Street Journal told you. Those are perfectly fine organizations, but this is your money. And your life.

One of the most important ways to zig is with your investments. Investors know that every market upturn will eventually be followed by a downturn. And the reverse is also true.

The secret is in the timing. And almost no one ever gets it exactly correct. Bulls and bears end up partying together eventually. If you knew the Dow had peaked at about 14,164 in October of 2007, you could have shifted your assets out. If you knew it had bottomed out at 6,547 and change in 2009, you would have made a fortune plowing your money back in.[27] None of us is that wise, including me. There are billions of bits of investment data that help determine where the market will go. It's impossible to zig or zag instantly, hundreds of times a day. Even if you could manage that successfully, handling it would eat you alive. Image you are sitting at a roulette table. That pile of chips in front of you is your entire life savings. Once you push some chips onto the table, you are gambling you will lose them. Place them on a single number, like you would buying a stock, and it could come up big.

Or you could lose it all. I'm a financial advisor and the thought of my clients losing their money has always made me physically ill. It should do the same to you. You could scrimp and save every spare dime for a year and lose it all in an instant. Most of my clients aren't comfortable with that kind of gambling. And when they do it, they are careful. That means even if you want to gamble in the markets, don't gamble with everything. Embrace the gains you make and take some, most or all of that money off the table. Or maybe you'd rather not gamble at all. If that's your response, you're learning.

7.

Blue Suede Shoes

'VE MET PLENTY OF famous people in my life—singers, actors, presidents, governors, senators and congressmen. I've only met one man called The King.[28]

I met him in person in 1971, and he was every bit as good-looking as you'd think. Here the most charismatic person anyone in the room had ever met walks in, just after a concert in Dallas. There were probably a hundred people in the room and it just went completely quiet like the pope had entered.

Only he didn't act like he was The King. He walked around the room for maybe ten minutes, quiet and unassuming. He just wandered around shaking hands with the people there—the mayor, a local congressman and other big wigs—and everybody seemed small in comparison. I got to shake his hand and it was funny because he introduced himself.

I saw him again a few years later when he was on tour. This time I was in the audience. I reached out to James Burton and asked his help getting three tickets to the show—for me, my not-yet-wife Susan and my future mother-in-law.

The show was in May, just a month before our wedding. I knew James wouldn't let us down. We got tickets for both shows, front row center. The 2 p.m. performance was incredible and I figured both Susan and her mother had to be impressed. Only that wasn't enough. I'm a Texas boy and we have to show off to our women folk when we get the chance.

I walked up to the stage as the crowd began to filter out. I flagged James down and asked if he could do me another favor. I pointed to Susan and her Mom, Nella, and explained that I needed to score points with the future family. He called another guy over and said, "Charlie's the guy you need." So Charlie comes over and I explained the situation. Charlie took a pen and wrote a note on his hand. I figured there was no way that was going to survive to the next show. I just hoped and prayed it would.

We left to go get dinner and raced back in time for the 8 p.m. performance. We were seated in exactly the same spots and I could tell Mrs. Hanes was already pretty pleased. Elvis came out and was doing an amazing show. When he got to his signature moment where he was giving out the scarves, Charlie motioned to our seats. Elvis gave her a scarf and got down on one knee, kissed her on the cheek and told her that she reminded him of his momma.

I was in like Flint.

It helped get me inspired for what was to come—performing as The King, not just listening to him.

The life of an Elvis Tribute Artist (That's the term we're all supposed to use these days,) is strange. Most artists do it as a part-time thing, not a lifestyle. It still sets you apart. It's strange and you know it. That world ends up being more a collection of oddball anecdotes than it does a career.

You end up creating your own costumes, buying replicas of jewelry and other items he wore on tour. Some guys change how they wear their hair and grow the sideburns to look authentic. I certainly grew out my sideburns some.

My entry into the world of Elvis Tribute Artists began at a church party where I was asked to entertain. I sang three or four Elvis songs, doing my best to sound like The King without the pelvis moves! After the party, one of my friends approached me and said, "Wow! You really sound just like Elvis!" That started me thinking. I had been singing his songs since high school, but it suddenly dawned on me that there was a whole world of opportunity out there that I had not even imagined. My mind began to race through the possibilities.

One essential item is the costume. The first one I purchased was handled over the phone. The business that did the work would have you send in your measurements and they'd create a shell of the outfit and send it back to you for resizing. Once that was done, you'd return it and they handle the rest—sewing in a liner, adding whatever adornment was called for on that particular suit. Elvis never had a suit with sequins—only metal studs or semi-precious stones that created his special designs. The costumes are all surprisingly heavy. I don't know how the man ever gained weight. (I guess those fluffer-nutter(29) sandwiches he liked so much packed on the pounds.)

One night after performing at a private party, I got asked about some of the accessories. So I started finding places to purchase little accents to the outfit. As it got more and more serious, I was asked to perform in a show as the '70s Elvis with another guy doing the '50s Elvis.

This was before the days of digital recordings. So I had a nice tape set up but it was harder to figure out where you were, harder to be specific about your spot in the song. As I'm walking in, people slow me up, one couple takes a picture. I can hear the music but I don't have a clue where we were. So I grabbed the mic and just started rocking it out, did an hour show and got rave reviews.

The owner loved us and asked us to do two shows each year. He also invited me to serve on the board and that was just icing on the cake. I started doing Elvis twice a year at those shows and naturally I did other performances in between as both Elvis and Johnny Cash.

That led to a project we called the Sun Record All-Stars. It was me and my buddy Mike doing a mixture of classic country greats. I opened the show with Johnny Cash. And then he'd do Jerry Lee Lewis. He would pound on the keyboards like he was playing while our keyboard player made the sounds.

Mike would follow with Roy Orbison. He's funny and he would always make the crowd laugh. It was weird because I knew Roy and it reminded me of the vice presidential debate where the line was, "I knew John Kennedy" only Mike sang Roy so well it was scary.

At the time, I hadn't heard him perform. He stepped up to the microphone and I didn't know what to expect. When he started to sing, I got the chills. I called Susan and told her to get over to the show because she had to see him. I ended it with The King. The crowd went nuts.

Once people heard of our Friday show, we sold out Saturday night. The manager asked us back and we sold out the next weekend as well.

Over time, we developed another show called "Just '50s Rock 'n' Roll." We mixed in another West Texan, Buddy Holly, along with Neil Diamond, Ricky Nelson and Bobby Darin to go with some of the other standards of Elvis and Roy. With that much variety, we could mix and match songs and always entertain the crowds.

That was about the time I was encouraged to enter the national contest in Branson among Elvis artists. I looked it up online, submitted a picture and a CD of me singing just to get considered. Two weeks later they called to say I was one of the fifty-one men chosen in the United States to compete.

I could hardly wait.

Branson was an experience. They divided us into three groups of seventeen. Each performer was to get six minutes on stage. You had to have the music prerecorded. There was no live music, just singing. I figured everyone would sing the same predictable Elvis songs—"Suspicious Minds," "Hound Dog" and other big hits. I knew I had to stand out to win. I decided to lead with Elvis' version of "You Gave Me a Mountain," and follow with "Such A Night," and "Kentucky Rain" as my main songs.

Incredibly, I made the cut. I was one of the fifteen that moved on and I could tell some of my competitors weren't happy. These were Elvis artists who didn't ever leave character off stage. They came from all over the country. Some of them even worked Vegas as Elvis. They looked like him, they dressed like him, and they talked like him all the time. I was just a part-time Elvis. It was all pretty freaking weird.

But not weird enough to stop me.

I didn't win. The top five were all professionals. I tied another Elvis for seventh. I wasn't good enough to be The King, but I sure felt like one.

Being Elvis can take you almost anywhere, even to the hospital. I was performing in Baltimore at the Marriott Hotel working with the Navy. I was watching Texas on TV and the football game started going poorly. The next thing I knew, I was having chest pains.

I had my show that night and I wanted to stick it out. I didn't think it was anything serious. I made it downstairs and I'm talking to someone. The next thing I knew, the ambulance was there taking me to the University of Maryland Medical Center.

They roll me through into the emergency room and have a hard time getting a reading on my heart. They wheel me into the Cardiology Department and hook me up to enough wires to light a football stadium.

I'm lying there with wires coming out of everything except my nose and backside. They're treating me for a potential heart attack and I'm in bed between two other beds. First this young woman is in the bed left to me. And they come in and work on her, desperately trying to save her. Only they can't. And before they can move her, they bring in a man and put him on the other side of me. And they lose him, too.

No other word for that than terrifying. It really helped my morale when they moved me to another room.

Around 1 a.m., two doctors came by. I remember them because they reminded me of Bill Cosby and Robert Culp from the old "I Spy" TV shows. I'm stuck in the bed, wires everywhere and they wanted to do a rectal exam. Now, I know it's a teaching hospital, but I had to remind them in graphic language that was one part of my body that was functioning just fine.

I was lucky. And I might joke about the doctors, but the hospital took good care of me and it turned out it wasn't my heart.

No matter how much you live your life as Elvis, you start gathering Elvis memorabilia. It starts out with just your stage gear—the white jump suit, a bit of jewelry, some sunglasses. But before you know it, you have several outfits for different occasions and eras.

It can get really expensive.

There's the amber gold vine suit. Or maybe the Phoenix suit with the red-and-blue phoenix. It's plain gorgeous. Most of the suits are worth at least $1,500 each. Many go for $2,500 or more. Throw in some white boots and you are just getting started.

I have pounds of jewelry—rings and pins and belt buckles, each one more sparkly than the last. The belt buckles are some of the glitziest items I own. I have both silver and gold replicas of the massive belt buckle given him by the Las Vegas International Hotel for setting a world championship attendance record.

If I laid it all out on the floor and hit it with lights, I could blind half of Midland.

I carry my Elvis travel bag to every show with the appropriate extras. There's the Hawaiian lei, lots of the jewelry and, of course, the scarves that I hand out just like he did. Except mine are signed, "Dee Carter as Elvis." The ladies still love them.

Then there's the knickknacks. I have piles of Elvis memorabilia scattered across my office and stacked up in a storage space. Many of the items were gifts from friends and clients. I have a small replica Elvis car, the Christmas decorations, the decanters and enough goodies to fill a wing at Graceland. If the people at the Franklin Mint ever want to find samples of all the Elvis plates they've made, I know just where to look.

There's even a little Elvis teddy bear that plays music.

I have this Elvis statuette depicting Elvis on a surfboard that I picked up after a show in Switzerland. I like it, but I love the story behind it. A company hired me to do a performance in Switzerland.

I had no idea what to charge. My Elvis life doesn't typically take me overseas. So they gave us two days in London and two days in Paris, along with the trip to Switzerland.

The performance was in one of the finest hotels[30] in Montreux. The hotel was actually built around an old opera house that had been upgraded with state-of-the-art sound. I don't think the real Elvis would have gotten better.

There were hundreds of seats and only about two hundred of them were filled. I'm on the fourth or fifth number and I'm really into it. It was such a great venue and I could see the crowd was rocking out to every song.

The stage manager motions to me between songs and asks if I would mind if other people could come in. Apparently, the sound system was so good that they could hear it outside. And the people must have liked what they heard.

I told him it was fine with me. People started flooding in. They took all the seats. Some people were standing along the sides. We filled the room and then some. When I was done, the applause was worth the trip.

The next day, Susan and I were walking down the street, and went into a convenience store. I saw in the corner of the store there were two tribute areas to celebrities. I looked in the corner and there was a tribute to Elvis and Freddie Mercury. The band Queen with Freddie Mercury used to record in Switzerland and he's a big deal there. They even have an annual "Freddie Mercury Montreux Memorial Day" every September.

Over in the other corner was the Elvis display. I liked this one item and the store owner came over and told me he wasn't going to get any more. He had lost his contract to carry the merchandise. I told him I would try to help him and as we got talking he started telling me about how he had heard this great Elvis artist at the opera house the night before.

I had Elvis style sideburns at that point and I'm looking at him and it dawned on him he had heard me sing. He thanked me and gave me the item as a souvenir.

The Swiss were all like that. They treated us great.

I love all the items I've gathered over the years—from across two different continents. But one Elvis likeness is more special than all the rest.

I have a client I have known since high school. She's a fantastic lady who has overcome amazing hardships. She lost her husband and two grandchildren in a disastrous accident. She was burned badly though she survived because she was thrown clear through the windshield and away from the crash.

I went to see if I could help her while she was recuperating. I knew she wasn't up to dealing with all of the bureaucratic things required when loved ones pass away. She was still stranded in a hospital bed and these things needed to be handled. I was able to sort through the whole mess, the insurance payments, lawyers and taxes and give her the peace of mind that was necessary while she was trying to recover. I've been working with her ever since.

After she recovered, she decided to open a bed-and-breakfast. She called me because I was scheduled to perform at the grand opening. She wanted to make sure I stopped by her house because she had a gift for me. She told me she had a picture she'd been trying to get an antique store to part with for years. The owner finally sold it because she needed the money. I figured it was just another picture of Elvis. I cared more about the thought behind it than what I assumed would be another generic picture of The King.

The turnout for the event was great—maybe three-fourths of the town showed up. Then came the picture. She kept telling me about how it had a special soul in it. I looked at it and thanked her, but I didn't really pay too much attention to it until I got back.

I really appreciated the image and picked a nice spot on the wall for it. But one of my clients examined it one day and told me she didn't think it was a print, that it was a very well-done pastel. She thought it was an original. My client started pointing out the artist's strokes and other details I hadn't noticed before.

I called my friend and asked her about the print and its origins. She told me the dealer had purchased it from an estate sale. Next, I researched the image because I knew I had seen the picture before. I know my Elvis. Turns out there are two similar pictures and those led me back to the talented artist who did it.

My email to her generated a prompt response talking about how some of her drawings had been turned into prints. I'm certain she figured that's what my inquiry was about. She asked the dimensions of the image and when I told her she followed up with a request for a photo.

That's when things got interesting.

The artist gave me a call and asked me if I would do her a small favor. She wanted me to take down the picture and cut a tiny hole in the backing right near the top. I cut the paper with my little Swiss Army knife, which I actually purchased in that shop in Switzerland, and I saw a little image there. She asked what I saw and I told her there was a picture of a bowl of bread with red, green and blue flowers.

It sounded like she gasped on the other end of the line. That was the picture she sold in 1975. It was an original, probably worth $25,000 to a collector. There was only one hitch. (Isn't there always?) I needed a certificate of authenticity. And the artist wouldn't provide one without me first signing away rights to the image. That didn't work for me. I would have liked the official record, but it's not like I'd ever sell it. I love the picture. And the gift and the gift-giver are too special to me to ever sell.

Even though the artist and I didn't and couldn't come to an agreement, she's still fantastic at what she does. She takes a photograph of someone famous like Robert Redford and produces the best likeness you can imagine. She's done it for a whole bunch of different celebrities. The one I have hanging now in my office is the best likeness of Elvis I've ever seen.

I reached a point where I was doing lots of Elvis shows, maybe twenty shows a year. I went everywhere in West Texas in one of those jumpsuits. I actually performed a wedding in one of them. (It sounds like a goofy request, but the couple is still together.) Elvis became one of my signatures and I still get introduced as Elvis all the time.

You have to play the part, though I never made a dime on any of it. All the money went to the Cystic Fibrosis Foundation or the Honor Flight.[31] I paid the musicians, back-up singers. The rest of my share went to charity. Any charity willing to share that way, I would do their show.

I was driving back from Odessa one night. I had done a show at the Odessa Country Club. I packed up my car and drove back to Midland. The trunk was jammed tight with all my gear—sound equipment, guitar, the works. My Elvis go bag was in the front next to me, jammed with more trinkets. I had jewelry and Elvis scarves packed together with my wallet and license. And I was wearing my baby blue Elvis jumpsuit and sunglasses. Hadn't left character.

I'm tooling along down the highway when the red-and-blue lights go off behind me. I thought to myself, this is going be fun. The officer comes up alongside the car, takes one look at me and says, "Oh my God!" I put on my best Elvis voice and responded, "Yeah, baby, you got me now."

I took off the sunglasses and tried to get serious and asked him what I had done. He still had a grin on his face but he told me my license tag light was out. I learned from him that drug dealers do that to hide the tags, so the officer was looking for a drug smuggler, not an Elvis Tribute Artist.

I got out of the car and he must have known no drug smuggler goes dressed like this. So he asked me if he could get a photo. I said sure and stood in front of the police car with my arm around him, smiling. Afterward, I opened the trunk and sure enough, one of the things I had jammed in there had knocked the bulb loose.

He told me, "I can't wait to get back to the station and tell everybody that I stopped Elvis tonight." Most likely the boys in blue got quite a laugh out of that one.

It's amazing how many different kinds of people love Elvis. They're from all walks of life. One time I was driving down the streets of Midland heading to St. Stephens Church to perform for a Catholic priest's 70th birthday. A guy saw me, made a U-turn and followed me all the way to the church.

When I climbed out of my car, he walked over to me and said, "I have to know what's going on. I see Elvis driving down the street and I have to know." I told him about the birthday party and he wanted to join in. I asked, "Are you Catholic?" He shook his head no with a sheepish look. I chuckled and said, "Neither am I. So now, you're my manager." I didn't even know the guy but he loved Elvis, so I had to invite him.

The priest didn't know anything. He was caught completely by surprise. I was all set up in the hall and he had a nice chair right by the stage. I started performing and he loved it. In walked the bishop from San Angelo. He's a little guy, maybe 5'3", but he's wearing an enormous silver crucifix that hung down all the way to his waist.

He walked on up to the front and everybody got quiet. It's the bishop after all. But I'm in character. I'm Elvis. So I stopped him and pointed to the crucifix: "Hey baby, you can't come up here like that. You've got more bling than me."

Everybody laughed—the bishop, the priest, the congregation. I kept on going. I pointed to the priest and told him he had to move. "He outranks you, baby." They loved it. The bishop told me later that he wished everybody would treat them like that, that it made it much more real.

Every Elvis Tribute Artist travels. It's a must. Of course you go to Graceland. It's almost a pilgrimage and I've been there five times. It's a crazy place because Elvis lived such a crazy life.

During one trip, we also went to the 30th annual Elvis Presley Revue at the Comcast Theater in Memphis. It was a live performance, live band and all the guys who played with Elvis. The lineup included the Sweet Inspirations who had been his back-up band for nearly ten years. There was James Burton playing lead guitar, Jerry Scheff on bass, and Ron Tutt banging on the drums. And on the big screen was an enormous Elvis singing his heart out.

I had a VIP pass and I got behind the scenes and it was fascinating. The people who came to that show. Everybody was caught in the '60s.

There were Priscillas, Elvi and they all looked like they had stepped out of a time warp.

It's actually a good metaphor for people who have had Elvis as part of our lives for so long. You don't ever retire from Elvis. You just kind of slow down.

DEE'S DIRECTIVES:

Market History, History Repeats Itself.

I keep referring to the stock market as gambling. There are good reasons for that description. Because stocks in good companies can go down when the market goes down. It's not logic, it's herd mentality.

And it's been going on as long as the markets have been around. The philosopher George Santayana said those who ignore history are doomed to repeat it. I know he's correct when it comes to the stock market because I've read the best historical analysis of the market I've ever seen. I'm talking about my buddy Dave Scranton's analysis of the stock market through its history.

Talk to most advisors about the stock market and they will discuss how it's trending over the last five, ten or twenty years. Most might remember all the way back to the dotcom crash in 2000—just 18 years. The older ones might go back to the crash of 1987.

The easily available investment data are just as bad. Online charts from Google or Yahoo Finance give you a few decades of time horizon. Dave Scranton went back just a bit more—to the market's founding in 1792.

What he discovered isn't just astonishing. It's essential. The stock market has a rhythm just like a song. And just like a song, it repeats. There are bull market and bear market cycles.

Journalists and stock pickers toss around the term "bear market" like it's just a few years and you have to grin and bear it. Only that's just not true. A secular bear market cycle can last decades and you'll see the up-and-down and think the market is moving. Only at the end you're still where you were at the beginning.

Investors are told to invest in those times because the market will return 9 or 10 percent over time. But 2 or 3 percent of that is dividends. The rest is stock appreciation and there are long gaps where those stocks don't do much of anything.

Dave's analysis showed that there were periods like 1899 to 1921 or 1966 to 1988 where the stock market was largely flat. The biggest drop in stock market history—the Crash of 1929—set in motion a period from 1929 to 1954 where the market whipsawed some and ended up where it started.

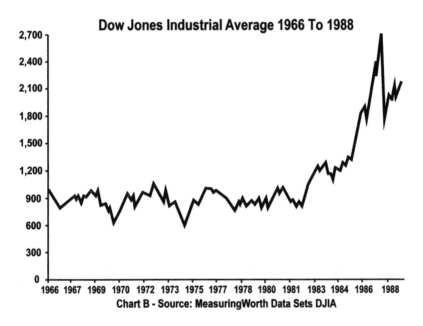

Dow Jones Industrial Average 1966 To 1988

Chart B - Source: MeasuringWorth Data Sets DJIA

Are you ready for a stomach-churning investment period lasting twenty-five years? I know you didn't say yes to that. As I write this, the market is up nearly four times higher than it was in 2009. That sounds astonishing, unless you remember how far it fell to get there.

Assume you rode the market all the way down and back all the way up, maybe it's time you took your money out of the casino, took your profits and found a simpler way.

The author Terrence "VP Pappy" Murphy writes about poker but I stumbled across a quote of his that applies to the stock market, as well. "A gambler never makes the same mistake twice. It's usually three or more times." The same could be said of investors.

8.

I've Been Everywhere

LIKE THE CHAPTER TITLE says, I've been everywhere. Oh, not literally. I haven't traveled to Antarctica. There's not a lot of need for either financial advice or Elvis tribute artists there, I imagine.

But I have been traveling most of this beautiful land of ours and around the globe for my entire life. I think the travel bug bites you when you live in a foreign land at a very young age. Only this isn't a travelogue. You need to travel not just to experience the world, but to understand it.

We are more interconnected globally now than ever before. That means opportunities for exciting travel for people who could barely afford to go out of state decades ago. It also means jobs, business opportunities and investments. If you want to begin to grasp that, you need to understand the world not just from TV, movies or books. You need to see it, live it and talk to people about it.

Early in my career, I worked for a small insurance company with its home office in Arlington, Texas. One of the most-common benefits for working with insurance companies, at that time, was traveling to other places for "company meetings." That made them tax deductible to the company. It was one of the few times in life where I knew people looked forward to meetings.

Our first trip was to Mexico City in 1972, which was a real eye-opener. That was only four years after Mexico City hosted the Olympics, so I was shocked how bad it was. If you want to learn how nice we have it in America, just visit any third-world nation. I learned what that term really meant because it was my habit to get out and visit with the locals whenever I had the chance. (Susan and I still do this. Ordinary people are good all over. Sometimes those who tell them what to do aren't.)

Mexico was one of the saddest experiences I have ever had. It's a lovely country and the people were truly kind to me. But the poverty is horrendous and the elite were, by any standards, quite well-to-do and oblivious to the differences. Liberals complain about the divide between rich and poor in the United States. They need to travel next door to see what that really means. The poor in America have cell phones and cars. In much of the rest of the world, they live in squalor and survive on what they can scavenge.

That trip definitely had an influence on how I deal with my clients today. It combined with what my Dad taught me about treating all people fairly. Now, I have folks that I work with from nearly all income levels and tax brackets. Every single one of them gets treated the same because every single one of them matters to me.

I have learned that those who have the least sometimes need more attention than those who have the most. Because the ones with the most to lose are the ones who have so little. If you have saved for years and have only $10,000 to invest, a slight market correction could leave you with very little and no easy way to recoup your losses. They might be oil field workers, or rough necks, as we call them here in Texas, or waiters and waitresses, scrimping just to save a few bucks each payday. They want to invest in ways where they don't lose what took them so long to earn.

That's why Mexico's system is messed up. It simply doesn't allow movement from one economic bracket to another. So, while I oppose illegal immigration, it's often caused by lack of economic opportunity. Blame The Powers That Be in Mexico for that.

Once I was done visiting our neighbor to the south, it was only logical that I'd want to travel north. After Susan and I married and I had begun my work with Lincoln Financial, we qualified for a trip to Montreal, Canada.

The economic comparison between north and south of the border was quite astonishing. The two were almost complete opposites, though I had issues with both of them.

Montreal was clean and prosperous. Old Montreal was especially enchanting. The clock tower there honors the memory of lost sailors and serves as a welcoming beacon to the harbor. It's getting close to hundred years old now and looks just like someone moved Big Ben from London to the new world. And the Notre-Dame-de-Bon-Secours chapel catches the light at sunset in a way you just can't forget.

Canadians were much like Americans in the way that they saw the world, but with a leftward tilt. Their socialized medicine and socialist style government were the big difference. I didn't like how they allowed their government to make a lot of the decisions that Americans make for themselves and take for granted.

I learned more about who Americans are and who I am by being in another country and seeing my conservative political values challenged than I did staying in Texas.

I won't bother to list all the places Susan and I have been. We've either been to or through most of the countries in North America and Europe. We've visited many of the Caribbean islands and much of the Mediterranean by cruise ship and got to see numerous sights we might have missed with more point-to-point travel.

The Mediterranean cruise was unique because it took us not just too beautiful places, but brought history to life. Rome, Pompeii, Athens, Ephesus and Istanbul, and some other smaller towns like Rhodes, were no longer just place names from a textbook. They each took on special meaning.

That was in 2012, before the economic and governmental failures really seized hold of Greece. Our trip to the Acropolis was memorable and it's certainly the signature image of any travel there. But it was the visit to the Areopagus[32] or "Mars Hill" that I most recall. I had only read of Mars Hill (the name the Romans gave it) in the New Testament when Luke mentions it in the Acts of the Apostles.

That was the place that the apostle Paul preached to the people in the marketplace looking down from the hill. In Acts 17:24 he told the Greeks that, "The God who made the world and everything in it is the Lord of heaven and earth and does not live in temples built by human hands." He explained to those assembled that, "He has set a day when he will judge the world with justice."

To be there in the same place that Paul had preached truly touched me. Mars Hill is a huge outcropping of granite that is about fifty yards long, with a set of carved stairs to the top of the hill. (There's a more-modern set of stairs as well, but what's the thrill in that?) It was the site where Athens judges met so when Paul spoke of "justice" it was intended to resonate with his audience.

Mars Hill overlooks the old marketplace. I couldn't get over that I was standing on the same spot that Paul had stood, looking down into the old marketplace, and could actually read the plaque at the base of the steps. (It's not often I give thanks for my four years of Greek at Abilene Christian.)

The plaque told Paul's story, lifted straight from Acts. I couldn't help but feel a special presence as I stood there and recalled the biblical story. It's a site that has a profound meaning to Christians because Paul was teaching that Jesus had saved everyone, not just the Jewish people. He was welcoming everyone into the young faith.

It was the same feeling that I had three days later standing in the coliseum in Ephesus, Turkey. It had been built first by the Greeks but expanded by the Romans to handle up to 25,000 people. It's still tough for me to grasp that such things were constructed in the ancient world.

It was there that two Macedonian Christian men, Gaius and Aristarchus, were subjected to a show trial in front of a howling mob that could have numbered in the thousands. These companions of Paul were undaunted and defended their faith despite incredible odds against them.

The mob had dragged them there because of their connections to Paul. His disciples kept him out of Ephesus, so he was safe.

I try to picture Gaius and Aristarchus, how they looked facing the crowd howling for blood in that large coliseum. What courage they demonstrated. What faith! I have often wondered, over the years, if I could have shown that kind of courage in the face of what might have meant certain death.

Instead, their faith saved them. A brave city clerk confronted the crowd and calmed them, reminding them these two men had done no harm. They were able to walk away unharmed and rejoin the apostle Paul.

I got that same chill that I felt on Mars Hill while standing there on the marble stage of what is sometimes called the Great Theater. I still get that feeling when I recall those two stops on our voyage.

This is why travel is worth saving for. This kind of trip is priceless.

You've probably guessed at my love of history. Susan tries to placate it and when we travel, historical sites are always on the itinerary. If you know the past, then the present is easier to understand and the future simpler to predict.

Visiting Europe is a glimpse at all three. It's the origin for much of what we have in America and yet it shows the problems we face now or will in coming years.

Our trip to Montreux started with a free, two-day jaunt to Merry Old England. We devoted those two days to London—nowhere near enough time to see what we wanted to see. Most of that time was spent on the top of a double-decker tourist bus driving through the city seeing the sights. I always like to get out and walk when I can, but we didn't have the time.

We did get to stop for lunch at the Original Hard Rock Café, only to have our waitress tell us that she was from Montana. Hardly the classic English experience. But it was another lesson about how global our world has become.

We ate at a small pub the first night, within walking distance from the palace. We were the only tourists and the locals made quite a fuss about having two Texans there for dinner. The meal was OK, the people made it much more enjoyable.

I don't think you should visit London without seeing the changing of the guard at Buckingham Palace. It's like visiting Washington and not seeing the guards change at the Tomb of the Unknowns. Both are essential for their history and sense of honor.

The crowds around the palace were immense. We had pushed forward to within six feet of the guards, near the main gate. While I watched the well-trained men wearing the giant bearskin hats, I listened to the voices of those around us. We were surrounded by Americans from at least four or five states. I think tourism is the same everywhere. Locals don't appreciate what we have as much as those from far away.

Americans might have thrown off our royal yoke, but it doesn't mean we aren't still fascinated by regal trappings. Just ask Prince William and his lovely bride Kate. Americans are obsessed with the cute couple.

The trip from there to France was an exercise in rapid transit, something of a fantasy for a nation as large as ours. We took the Chunnel Train under the English Channel—flying through the French countryside at around 120 mph. Fast for group travel, though I know Texans sometimes take our roads at nearly that speed.

We arrived in Paris on the second of June and, naturally, our young maître d' asked if we were in France for the D-Day ceremonies. They commemorate the landing June 6th every year. We had to be in Switzerland at that time, but I did explain to the young man that my Dad had been part of the liberation army that set France free.

I was surprised how sincerely he thanked me. "Please tell your father how very much we appreciate what the Americans did for our country in the World War II." The French have a bad reputation for being rude to Americans. It took one sentence for him to undo a lot of negative PR.

In fact, we were treated royally by the hotel staff, who went out of their way to set up dinner at a restaurant within walking distance of the hotel. The young French woman who ran it was also the chef and she prepared a special steak for me and a chicken plate for Susan. Both were fantastic.

The Louvre was closed, but we had all of Paris to amuse ourselves. We walked through the Luxembourg Gardens with all their beauty, past the octagonal pond with children playing with boats. That path took us all the way to the Eiffel Tower, about three or four miles from where we left our cab. It so dominates the skyline that it looked a lot closer than it really was. When we saw it, that area was wide open. Soon it will be surrounded with $36 million worth of bulletproof glass.

Like I said, Europe is grappling with problems we might well face ourselves.

I've heard the expression "Elvis is everywhere" and I certainly proved it that trip. I was doing a lot of Elvis shows so I had let my hair and sideburns grow in appropriate style. I was also wearing my Elvis sunglasses that day and when we approached a scarf vendor in the shadow of the Eiffel Tower, I could see him smile. He said, "Ze King lives!" as we walked toward him. I thought it was hilarious. Susan was a bit Elvised out at the time and didn't see the humor.

We left Paris, via "bullet train," on our way to Switzerland, where we took a small local train from Zurich to Montreux. Our trip ended with a four-day stay in Gstaad, Switzerland,[33] a quaint village high in the Alps also called "Christmas Village" by the locals.

No cars are allowed in the village and in the winter, the snow and lights make the town look like what you might think the North Pole looks like just before Santa departs on his Christmas Eve rounds. Even there, I joined in to sing with a local band each night in the pub area.

Gstaad had an almost fantasy feel to it. Another universal reality is that small towns are friendly all the world over.

You really can't talk about Europe without talking about Germany. It's the dominant player in both history and current events. Business doesn't happen without German bankers and its government sets the civil agenda for much of what the European Union does—good and bad.

Susan and I went to visit our former German exchange student in 2011. We spent one day on the coast of the North Sea and socialized with the people living there. Robin was in the final year of his doctoral studies. On the day that we arrived, his wife, Katja, had completed her studies for her PhD. That evening, during dinner, Robin asked, "Honey, would you pass me the salt?" To which she replied, "That's Dr. Honey, to you!" We all laughed and enjoyed the time we had together. Their love is a reminder of the best Germany or any nation has to offer.

The other impressions of Germany were when we went to Berlin. And they reminded us of the worst. It's disturbing to stay in a hotel in what had been East Germany before the wall came down.

With all of our freedoms, I can't imagine what it would be like to live under the yoke of communism. Even decades after it was pushed aside, remnants like the hotel survive. At least it was clean, though we expected no less in a German hotel. It was also plain and lacked some of the "niceties" one might experience in places that had been in West Germany.

We spent an entire day and Sachsenhausen,[34] a former German concentration camp just north of Berlin. It's not a tourist destination, but an important education. It had been opened just after Adolph Hitler came to power as chancellor of Germany. On that day, sixty thousand Jews, Christians and those who had opposed Hitler were imprisoned in the camp.

It was one of the most difficult days that I can ever recall in all of our travels. To see where thousands of people were imprisoned and murdered is difficult to take. The camp is surrounded by barbed wire and has a two story white entrance building that seems ominously plain. The gate marked in classic Nazi style with "Arbeit Macht Frei" ("Work sets you free.") In wrought iron.

It was a terrifying example of what happens when people use hate as an ideology and lose touch with their own humanity. I will never forget it. I pray none of us do.

Most of our travel is more uplifting. Our top-notch symphony chorale group, the Midland-Odessa Symphony & Chorale,[35] does five or six concerts a year and heads to Europe every other year. We sang in Austria, which gave all of us "The Sound of Music" flashbacks.

Then we had five stops in Italy. The group is mostly Protestants, but we were still thrilled to sing for the high mass on Sunday at St. Peter's at noon. I don't know how many people can say they've performed at a venue with such historical and religious significance. It was an enormous crowd, but respectful, quiet and attentive and made us feel very welcome.

We spent a whole day in the city of Assisi, a city with an active monastery that has been there since Saint Francis[36] established the order about eight hundred years ago in the year 1209 AD. Assisi is another spot that doesn't allow cars, so we had to walk around the city and it was like being dropped back into another age. We viewed the very humble home of St. Francis and visited his equally modest tomb.

We spent another day in Florence, where I was completely blown away by the Cattedrale di Santa Maria del Fiore[37] or the Cathedral of St. Mary of the Flower. The artwork and murals on display were fully as wonderful as what we saw in the Vatican Museum in Rome.

It's astonishing, the beauty that some men can create while others destroy with equal vigor.

Not all my travel was to other countries. I've been to most of the lower 48, and Alaska and Hawaii, and found something special in each place. Every time I go to another part of America now, I am reminded of Charlie Daniels' monologue about the wonders of our nation in, "My Beautiful America." We are truly one nation under God for all the wonders we have at our fingertips.

Another Lincoln Financial trip took us to the 50th state of that union—the island paradise of Hawaii. We spent ten days there: five on Kauai and five on Maui. It didn't matter whether we were on land, sea or air, the area was gorgeous. On land, we had the fabulous beaches and interior parks. We took a helicopter to tour the Kauai[38] volcano and took to the sea for whale and dolphin watching. Each sight was more amazing than the last.

Folks there could teach the rest of us about living a laid-back lifestyle. They just didn't work on pressure and schedules there. We especially enjoyed that business attire which was a flowered shirt and flip-flops. It was my favorite trip inside the United States.

There's a lot we could learn from that way of living. You don't allow your job or your investments to rule your life. I began to learn that, while you need to understand your investments, don't let them own you. The old saying that all work and no play make Jack a dull boy, comes to mind.

There is a balancing act to be considered when you are planning your retirement or just saving for the future. Fixating on your past mistakes (Boy, I wish I had invested in Microsoft from Day One) is as bad as sitting in front of your computer and doing day trades. Both suck the joy out of life.

And that's an essential part of life—making yourself and those around you happy. If you can't find joy and do the things that make you happy, why sit and worry about how you are going to get there during every waking moment? I try to encourage my clients and my friends to stop and smell the roses.

Like many Americans, I'm a bit of a mutt—mostly Scottish, Irish and English, with a smattering of Norse, some Cherokee and perhaps even Jewish blood. But the Scots-Irish is strong in me and many Americans. So Susan and I have made plans to visit those homelands and spend ten days in Ireland and Scotland with the Midland-Odessa Symphony Chorale. Our family's original name appears to have been MacCarter, but was changed to Carter when John MacCarter moved his family from Scotland to England in the late 1600s after clan rivalries during the Robert the Bruce era.

It's important to know our own past, not just our nation's history. And I believe we don't stop learning as long as we're above ground.

DEE'S DIRECTIVES:

Don't Ask Your Risk Tolerance. Ask Why Do You Want To Risk What You Spent Your Life Building?

I'm not much of a gambler. I've been to Vegas, of course. There isn't an Elvis fan worth his salt, who hasn't. I've seen the casinos and taken my turn at the tables. It's an amusement park for adults. Only you can lose your shirt in five minutes if you aren't careful.

Oh, they hide that fact and talk about how it's entertainment. There are lots of flashing lights to make it look like an amusement park. But you could take your entire life savings and plop it down at one of the tables and people might barely blink an eye. You could lose it all in one roll of the dice or spin of the wheel.

That's why I don't like to gamble. I have friends who play pools for the NCAA tournaments and, this being West Texas, there's some betting that takes place on local football games. None of us is going to buy a mansion or even a used car from our winnings and we aren't going broke if we lose. We're conservative that way.

It almost defies understanding that people who won't bet more than $100, then turn around and bet every cent they've ever made in the stock market—the biggest casino in human history. I know they do it because it's not betting; it's "investing."

Only that's just not true. Investing is when you analyze an asset such as a company and determine it's got an excellent future. So you put some money into it. That's like buying Apple in the early 1980s because you were convinced of the impact of home computing.

If you've read this far, odds are you have money in the stock market. Maybe a little or maybe even a lot—mutual funds, IRAs, pensions or even individual stocks. How much have you analyzed those investments? Have you spent hours comparing mutual funds? Or even the market itself?

Probably not. You've been told for most of your life that the stock market works for you over the long haul. That the dotcom crash and 2007-2009 market collapse are just part of doing business. That the risk is worth the reward.

Investors are convinced that's true until things go bad. They just plow their hard-earned into the Dow or NASDAQ and hope the stocks go up. They get shocked when they go down. We are conditioned to accept crazy market swings to get the benefit of the long-term market.

What if you don't want that level of risk?

Then you don't have to have to have it. The whole risk/reward equation is based on it being worth it to you to be in the stock market. Only it might not be. Yes, the market eventually turns. A bull becomes a bear and vice versa. That can take years. If your time horizon is shorter, that might be more risk than you want to embrace.

There's an important phrase to remember when it comes to investing: Never gamble what you can't afford to lose.

Being True
To Your Values

IF YOUR LIFE IS TO mean anything it needs to be based on values. If you want to enjoy that life, you need to have that core foundation.

I have several cores to my life—family, faith, community, my nation and, helping others. This section addresses that. It's what really makes me tick. I already talked about Abilene Christian, but I go more into the idea of giving back here that the school has helped teach me. Charity is a key component to keep all of us from turning into Ebenezer Scrooge.

Family gets to the heart of what I care about in my life. I don't care who you think of as family. It might be your coworkers; you best friend or your blood relatives. But family is an essential core so you can weather the storms of the world. So is faith. Faith sustains us even when everything else might look bleak. And no matter how great things are now, sooner or later a challenge will come your way. Faith will help you in good times and bad, as it has me.

My West Texas community is unique (God bless it) but it's one of hundreds or thousands of unique places in our country. Not one of them defines being America. Not one of them should be left out either. We aren't just the people in D.C., New York and L.A., who think they run things. And we aren't just the people in the places they think of as flyover country. We are a united country that makes up the United States.

If you really want to leave a legacy to be proud of, these core areas are ones you need to start with.

9.

Family Tradition

IWANTED THIS CHAPTER TO be about the importance of family and family life. It's one of the pillars of my own existence and it should be for you, as well. Faith, family and freedom are great words to live by.

I know I had all the right words. They escape me somewhat now.

As I was writing this book, hoping to leave a written legacy to help others live by, I had to cope with a loss of my own—my beautiful sister Kay. She went to heaven not long after her 70th birthday.

Kay was my little sister, and by little, I mean just exactly that. She was born September 9th, 1947, just after I entered the first grade. I was too young to remember much about the birth.

Parenting was harder then. There were no tests to determine what genetic issues your baby might have. Kay's birth and diagnosis of her having Down syndrome was a jolt to both Mom and Dad. They didn't know what to expect. We didn't even have the term Down syndrome then. They used other, more derogatory terms to describe children born with this defect.

Kay had mild to mildly severe retardation. She was slow in her physical development and was never as verbal as typical children. My younger brother Larry, who was only four when she was born, and I became her protectors during those early years.

I remember there was a neighborhood boy who was picking on her. As soon as I found out, I went out in the alley and whipped him but good. He was about twice my size, but sometimes size doesn't matter. He was picking on Kay. I was full of righteous fury and I just went and beat the tar out of him. He lived down the alley about half a block away from us and he never came back down our way again.

No adults got involved. There was no great meeting about bullying. It was solved just like that—Texas style.

My youngest brother, Robert, was born when Kay was just six years old and they grew up together. She loved Robert more than anyone. But, she was not above throwing him under the bus as siblings will do. Robert reminded me of a time when Kay would sneak out of her room at night and raid the refrigerator to steal cheese slices. She'd take them back to her room to eat as a special treat.

Mom was displeased. She discovered all of the wrappers in Kay's wastebasket and sternly warned her that she did not want to find those wrappers in her wastebasket ever again. Knowing Mom, I bet she figured the issue was settled.

It was... sort of. A couple nights later, Robert awoke to a strange sound in his room. He looked and there was Kay stuffing *his* wastebasket with cheese wrappers. She may have had some learning difficulties, but her logic was sound. It's funny after seventy years of life, that's one of my favorite stories about her.

As Kay grew older, she became the darling of the family. All of us doted on her. Dad literally hovered over her and protected her for as long as he lived. He vowed that she would never be placed in a protected living home and that we would take care of her as long as she, or he, lived.

He lived up to that vow and it wasn't easy. We just didn't have a support network to help. We had family. Sometimes that's all you need.

Kay never attended school, but she did receive some early childhood assistance from the new special education program in Monahans when she was only twelve years old. That was a start. Later, when my parents moved to Midland, she was kept at home and her educational process slowed to a grinding stop.

It's difficult to explain how things were then with special needs patients. There weren't any resources to speak of—few books, no internet and little sophistication about coping with the problems. Every family had to make do by themselves. And we did the best we could.

Kay stayed in my parents' home until long after Dad's death in 1985. It took Mom's accident in the year 2000, while visiting my brother in California, to change things. We were keeping Kay with us at our home. It was a challenge to care for her and keep her engaged while I was working so much. It wasn't good for her.

When Susan learned that Mom wouldn't be coming back to Midland for at least three months, she searched for a place where Kay could spend the day with other learning disabled people. It was important for Kay to have a life outside of our home and this was the time to do it.

Susan discovered the Rock House, a fabulous series of group homes across Texas. Rock House helped Kay gain a certain degree of independence as a "temporary" resident for more than twenty years.

When Mom returned from California, she was, at first, pretty ticked off at how we had found a place for Kay. That soon turned into a real thankfulness and Susan deserves all the credit.

It was a new start. Kay had friends. Kay had a life of her own. She even had a boyfriend for the first time in her life. It was a transformation. She lost weight and her health improved markedly under the oversight of the professional care-givers at Rock House.

She remained a resident of Rock House until three years ago, when she fell and severely broke her fibula and had to have surgery. She never returned to her group home. Instead, she went into rehab and lived at the rehab center for the last three years of her life.

Her health began to decline. She was diagnosed with Alzheimer's in 2015, and passed from this life on October 26, 2017, at the age of seventy. Kay outlived most people with Down syndrome. That's a tribute to my family and to the marvelous people at Rock House.

My two brothers and I administered at her funeral with all three of us telling stories and singing three of our favorite hymns. Robert, who is pastor for a small Baptist church in Grove, Oklahoma, and I conducted the services.

People from our church and the Rock House family were in attendance. There were laughs and there were tears all honoring and remembering our "special Kay-Kay." She was buried next to her Mom and Dad. Dad is still watching over his little girl.

Death can teach us a lot about life, I suppose. It's usually hard to notice because we are caught up in grief. First, it's essential to remember that death is part of life. It sounds flip, but none of us is getting out of this life alive.

And we shouldn't want to. There is a point to this life and it has to do with our afterlife. I am confident that Kay is in Heaven with my parents now. That gives me comfort.

It also reminds me that life is for the living. That means do the right things—work hard, raise your family, save for a rainy day. (Hint: It always rains.) But try to enjoy yourself, enjoy your loved ones while you can.

Loved ones are family—an easy concept or a complicated one. It's made up of blood relatives who you might not know well and friends who you might think of as family because they are so close, so important.

My family started, as all families do, with my parents—my Mother Maurine and my Dad Dee. They gave me the education, the discipline and the love to grow up. It wasn't perfect. It never is. They gave me enough to build on for my own future.

They gave me a foundation. If you remember the Bible spoke a lot in those terms. Corinthians spoke in particular about how Jesus is the foundation for all things.

Losing Kay made me think about my parents. My Dad passed away on February 22, 1985, after his second major stroke. The first one nearly six years earlier had been devastating. It had left him paralyzed completely on his left side. Dad was no longer able to manage his business affairs.

That left us with no choice but to liquidate his automobile business. We sold thirty-three cars in about two or three weeks. Those were just vehicles. I really didn't know much about car sales, but it doesn't seem hard to do when you advertise that you will show the customer the invoice and the price is $100 over that figure.

Sadder still, we had to sell our seventeen horses and all of the tack that went with them. The horses were a more-complicated story. Horses are living, breathing beings. You don't just ride a horse. It's a partnership. Letting them go hurt.

I sold everything to a friend of mine from the Houston area who had told me that, if I ever wanted to sell that stallion, he would be a buyer. He agreed to take the eight brood mares, the six colts, Dad's riding horse, the stallion and the hateful English pony that Dad had bought for the grandkids to ride. (That was the one that kicked me in the chest soon after I returned to Texas.)

It wasn't just the horses. The eighty-acre ranch property needed a full-time worker. I couldn't do it and we didn't have enough money to pay a hand. By that time, I had signed on with Lincoln National Life as a manager-general agent and couldn't either care for the horses or the ranch and hold down my day job. We sold the ranch and bought Mom and Dad a nice little home in Midland in early 1979.

The house was smaller and better designed for Dad's limitations. With the horses and businesses gone, that meant less difficulty for everyone else—especially Mom. She cared lovingly for him for the next six years before his death at the tender age of sixty-eight. He would have been sixty-nine on April 20th of that year.

Dad's death was one of the biggest loses of my life. While I mourned the loss of my first marriage when the divorce took place, I have really never stopped mourning the loss of my Dad. He was the best man at Susan and my wedding and became my best friend.

We hunted together, rode horses together, cleaned out horse lots together, built horse pens together, dug ditches and planted oats together. The year we had when I returned to Texas in October of 1975 was incredible. It lasted until Dad had open heart surgery in December of 1976, with a stroke that followed one year later.

It was the happiest time of my life up till that moment.

While Dad wasn't able to work physically, his mind sharpened. It's like they say about how when you lose one sense, the others compensate. That was certainly the case with him. Dad was always sharp, but being laid up brought out a creative side in him that we had never seen.

He would lie in bed writing short stories on big, yellow legal pads. He'd think for a bit, scratch out some notes and then write away as the stories flowed from him to the pad. Over time, he filled nine entire legal pads with stories about the lives and adventures of Cherokee Indians. I never even knew that interested him.

He kept his mind busy even when he wasn't writing. He'd read, watch TV or intrude into our games of Trivial Pursuit. We'd be sitting in another room playing the game. Someone would read a question and Dad would shout out the answer before any of us could.

We'd always try to get him to play, but I think he liked it better this way. Dad had always been a hard-driving man and even toward the end, he kept driving. Only it was his mind he kept moving, not his body any more.

I still can't believe Dad is gone. This isn't meant to mean my Mom meant less to me. There's just something about boys wanting to be like their fathers, wanting their respect. She couldn't compete with that. No mother can.

My Mom continued to live in that little house in Midland for several years after Dad's passing. Eventually, her Rheumatoid Arthritis got worse and she became unable to care for the home and herself. We moved her into an assisted living place in the spring of 2000. She remained there until she needed full-time nursing care at age eighty-six. She passed away on September 16, 2008, and would have been ninety in January of the next year.

The women are tough in my family.

My rock is Susan. She keeps me steady. She helps me weather the storms. She's the reason my family has held together for more than forty-two years. This book is more than 60,000 words. I could write every one of them about her and not be finished. Or I could write a few and the whole world would understand how I feel.

I remember Jimmy Stewart in the movie "Shenandoah" explaining how a man has to both love and like his wife. I'm lucky because I do both. I also admire her for all she has handled over the years and the way she has handled it.

Susan and I were "caretakers" almost from the day we married. That's a lot to ask from anyone you marry. Dad had his open-heart surgery just six months after our wedding and, one year later, his first stroke. That meant a lot of time and commitment.

We were at the ranch or their home nearly every day over the next thirty-two years!

No, that's not an exaggeration. I am blessed to be married to a woman who not only took me on; she really became the matriarch of the family almost immediately. That role is one she filled wonderfully and still does today.

Susan serves as the guardian for our daughter, Erin, who also has Down syndrome. She filled the same role for my late sister Kay and I know it wasn't easy. I thank God for Susan and the strength that she has shown over these years. Everything I've been able to accomplish has been because of her.

The two of us have been together roughly forty-two years. It's funny, you spend that much time together and it's often not the big things that you dwell on, it's the little ones. I have my favorite picture of Susan where I think she looks so beautiful and cute that I can't get over it.

We were out visiting some clients of mine who happen to raise goats. And they had baby goats out in the pasture. The goats were hopping all over the place, jumping up on anything they could find. Susan asked if she could hold one. They said yes, but there's a problem.

There's almost no way to catch a baby goat if it doesn't want to be caught. It's like chasing a greased pig. I held up my phone to take a picture of what I thought would be a funny chase scene. Instead, she just walked out and picked up the little goat she aimed for. It didn't budge an inch, like it already knew her. I guess that maternal sense crosses species.

I couldn't tell which of them was happier, Susan or the goat. But I'm pretty sure it was Susan. She had this glow about her and she looked like the happiest woman in the world. I quickly took the picture with my phone and it's the best photo of her I've ever seen.

I thought Susan would never put down that goat. I was sure she wanted to come home with it. And when she finally did put it on the ground, the goat followed her everywhere like a little chick chasing after its momma.

That's Susan, strong when she has to be and child-like in her innocence around animals and children.

We have two daughters. Erin, our oldest daughter, is 39, and Mandee, our youngest. Growing up with Kay and having her in my life helped me with raising Erin. She was our first-born and the struggle was great. But my loving and lovely sister Kay helped teach us.

Kay and Erin both have helped make me more understanding and tolerant of the problems that my clients face day-to-day. Going from big brother to father of a child with a cognitive disability teaches patience, understanding and the meaning of unlimited love.

They both grew up with such pure hearts; it helped bring out the best in us. Susan and I have volunteered to serve as counselors for those parents who find themselves faced with this challenge. I have served on the Board of Directors for the Midland chapter of the Association for Retarded Citizens. I'm pretty sure national organizations don't use that word any more, but it is meaningful to those of us who have been and are still involved in the lives of so many people coping with this problem.

For years, I volunteered for the Special Olympics as a "hugger" and a "judge" and enjoyed every minute of the time that I spent working with the association. If you want your heart to grow three sizes like the Grinch, all you need to do is serve as a hugger once. The love and joy on those faces makes it all worthwhile.

Raising Erin opened that door to helping others. She's a big part of our family even though she lives in the Rock House like Kay had. We placed her there nearly twenty years ago, after seeing how it helped Kay live a better life. We knew Erin needed to live on her own, apart from me and Susan.

She's the apple of her Daddy's eye and makes me laugh a lot. She's got a great sense of humor and absolutely adores Elvis. Her grandmother watched her a lot growing up and Mom loved The King, too, and watched a lot of Elvis movies. It's a family addiction, I think.

And that takes me to my youngest—Mandee. What parent doesn't try to dote on their youngest child, even after they're an adult? Mandee became part of my retirement planning firm early in 2017 and I'm thrilled.

I've been so impressed with her, all that she has accomplished and overcome in her young life. I hope to leave the practice to her, but she has to earn it and I know she will.

Because she's proven to me impossible things just take her a bit longer, they don't stop her. Mandee was born with Cystic Fibrosis—an incredible challenge. Yet I've seen her fight it with all the strength of Muhammad Ali. She still has some health problems, but she combats things every day that I couldn't do, to keep her condition in check. It takes character to do all that, character that she brings to work every day.

She's smart as a whip and dedicated because she loves people so much. It's a natural gift for her. And, luckily for her, she also looks just like her mom, enough that you can't tell them apart in photos taken when they were close to the same age.

I'll be bragging on her more later in the book when I discuss my practice.

I'd be a rotten brother if I didn't mention Larry and Robert again. Larry is retired from NBC in California where he ended up getting his union license as a carpenter. That meant he worked for one of the greatest names in TV—Johnny Carson—and after him, the always-amusing Jay Leno. He finally retired and moved to the Dallas area where he is actively involved with the Turtle Creek Chorale, a two hundred-member men's group known nationally for their talent.

Robert, who is a Baptist pastor, also was a senior vice-president for Comcast Communications. He retired early and moved to Grove Oklahoma. The church congregation loved him so much they asked him to become their pastor when the original pastor retired. He had no formal religious training, but has, by all reports, done a fantastic job in the position.

I know it might sound strange, but my ex-wife Anne is still a part of my life, and, I hope she always will be. She and my current wife, Susan, are good friends and talk often on the phone. When my Father and my Mother passed, Anne came to the funerals and stayed at our home for the two days surrounding the events. When we go to Lubbock to see the grandchildren, we always call Anne and Sam to see if they would like to join us for dinner. Most of the time, they do as friends should.

Anne and I had two wonderful children and now three grandchildren as well. We're both proud of all of them.

Randa Lang, our oldest, and her husband, Jonathan, also live in Lubbock. Randa is employed by the school district as an accountant. Maybe numbers run in the genes. They both graduated from Lubbock Christian University. They are the parents of two of our grandchildren: Ashley, a senior at Friendship High School in Lubbock, and Brady, a sixth-grader. Both of them are part of the gifted and talented classes in Lubbock.

Ashley has recently been awarded the Presidential Scholarship at Abilene Christian University, my alma mater. That's as prestigious an award as it sounds, given only to a select few students. She will enter the university in the Fall of 2018, as a second semester freshman, due to her pre-college credits earned while in high school. Brady is following in her footsteps. I am obviously very proud of all of my grandchildren and their parents, who have given them the guidance and challenge to be the very best that they can be.

Devyn received his BA from Georgia State University in Atlanta and his MA from Emery University in Psychology and Anthropology. He is currently teaching Anthropology at Georgia State and doing some counseling with children on the side. He is also the father of our seven-year-old granddaughter, Lily. I'm sure if I redo this book in another decade, I'll be bragging on her academic achievements, too.

I've had a good life and my family has been a huge part of it. Watching Mandee and Erin grow up has been one of the high watermarks in my life. One of the great things about being a parent is the same when you are doing financial planning. It's all about bringing a person along—teaching, helping them grow and be their best. All the time, you are watching over them, keeping them safe.

You get to see the results of your work. I loved watching my children make mistakes and learn.

Each time, I'd try to recall my own parents and how they taught me. I loved being there when my first granddaughter was born. I loved holding her and being a Granddaddy. Those moments give you hope—for their future and even the future of all mankind.

I'm not a negative person at all. Everything good and bad that has happened has been part of my life. They were all, in some way or another, blessings from God. They are the things that make us who we are. And you need family to experience them.

DEE'S DIRECTIVES:

The Best Defense Is A Good Offense.

America has changed a lot since 1776. We now think of that expression in terms of football. Texans know better. We just have to visit the remains of a tiny mission sitting in the heart of San Antonio called The Alamo for a reminder.

Some 200 men including Davy Crockett, Jim Bowie and William Travis lost their lives defending Texas. They fought behind the adobe walls of their small fort while an army was being raised. The Battle of the Alamo was iconic. Those heroes fought and died so that Texas would have a chance to win the war. In less than a month's time after it fell, an army was assembled under Gen. Sam Houston and won freedom for Texas.

Defense works. Military people understand that. Many financial people are reluctant to admit it. Sure, at the high levels of finance, they grasp it. Hedge funds can be geared so that they protect assets, for example.

But much of market madness is designed to make money now. The time horizon is short-term, the returns must be immediate.

Let's talk about how that played out in the recent stock market. We've had two major market drops in just this millennium.

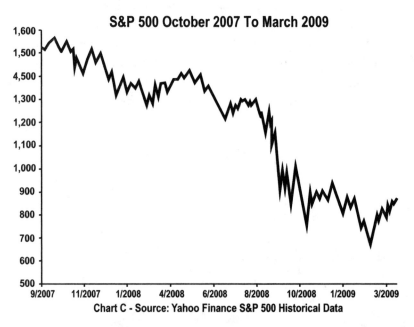

S&P 500 October 2007 To March 2009

Chart C - Source: Yahoo Finance S&P 500 Historical Data

The one you probably remember most was most recent. The S&P lost 55 percent in the 17 months from October 2007 to March 2009, according to MorningStar[39]. The stock crash set in motion the Great Recession. The crash before that was worse for some.

The tech heavy NASDAQ fell 78 percent from March 2000 to October of 2002, according to Wise StockBuyer. That's two major drops of 50 percent, one of them that went to 78 percent in tech.[40]

But, no one talks about what that truly means to investors.

Let's assume you have $1 million and the market drops 50 percent. You are down to $500,000 and need to double your money just to break even. It's actually more difficult than that. First there's inflation. Throw that in the mix and your problem just got worse. How much more you have to earn back depends on how long that recovery takes.

Only money isn't static for most of us. Few people have investment accounts with enough zeroes that they can just sit there and watch as the markets slowly begin to add value again.

Let's take that same $1 million and assume you are retired and you need it to pay your bills. You figure at 67, you can tap the investments for $50,000 a year and have enough to live on until you are nearly 90. Toss in your Social Security and you assume you are in a good position.

Only a market downturn comes and cuts your life's savings by 50 percent. You still need to tap that amount for $50,000 each year. If the market takes four years to recover, you've spent $200,000 you needed to rebuild. Your finances aren't repaired. Depending on when the recovery happened, you might have only seen appreciation on your remaining money. You aren't even back at Square One.

Historically, those kinds of downturns come in threes. I expect another one in the not too distant future. You should, as well.

10.

It Is Well
With My Soul

FAITH IS AN ESSENTIAL part of my life. Not because I am a minister. Anybody can be a minister. Just mail in your application and a few bucks and you are approved. But approved for what? You need to believe in something for religion to be real in your life. You don't need a piece of paper to do it.

I don't hide my faith. I try to live it. And sometimes that's a challenge to do. Life hits you hard sometimes. It can be overwhelming. It's times like that we need faith more, not less. I take my lessons in this not just from the Bible but from my favorite hymn, "It Is Well With My Soul."

It was written by Horatio Spafford in 1876. Just a few years before, he was a man who had an amazing life. He was married with five children and had extensive real estate holdings in Chicago. You could say he had it made. I imagine he might have thought so, as well.

Then his young and only son died. A short time later, the Chicago fire wiped out his real estate holdings, crushing him financially. He was determined to take his wife and four daughters to Europe by ship for a much-needed getaway. At the last minute, he had to stay behind to wrestle with zoning problems as he struggled to rebuild.

The ship, the SS Ville du Havre,[41] met with tragedy, slamming into another ship. His young daughters didn't survive. His poor wife Anna sent him this heart-wrenching message: "Saved alone."

He kept his faith despite those horrendous tragedies and wrote the hymn. It begins like this:

> "When peace, like a river, attendeth my way,
> When sorrows like sea billows roll;
> Whatever my lot, Thou has taught me to say,
> It is well, it is well, with my soul."[42]

Here's a man who had lost almost everything—his money, his children, his legacy. He was on his way to be with his wife in another ship yet he found peace in the waters, peace in his soul.

It has always meant a lot to me. I was given a gift of the song and it now hangs framed on my office wall. Like "Amazing Grace," it is one of the most-descriptive songs about how difficult life can be and yet both songs answer that we should turn to God in those times.

I firmly believe I discovered what God wanted me to do in life, helping others survive financially. That changed me over the years more than I imagined—both from the good times and the bad. I try to keep this song in my heart to remind me of the right path.

It's what this life is all about.

I was raised in a good ol' Southern Baptist home. Not a unique story south of the Mason-Dixon Line. My uncle was a Baptist preacher and I recall, as a boy, attending some of his revival meetings in our area of West Texas. Revival meetings were just that, a time for revival of faith.

I found myself sitting on the second row of the small country church where he held one of those meetings. People dressed up to go to church in those days. It was hot and we didn't have air conditioning. The revival meeting was packed, every pew filled and some men in shirt and tie standing in the back. Even now, it's not too hard to fill a church in West Texas.

I was just twelve, hanging out with three of my rowdy friends, not too interested in the proceedings. Then the chorus began the "invitation song," essentially a welcome to people to come up and announce their faith. It's a staple for the Baptist Church and almost any evangelical church.

I watched as all three of my friends got up and stepped out solemnly into the aisle, responding to the invitation. I didn't know what to do, so I followed, as any good sheep would do. I figured it was better to be with my friends than sitting alone in the pew.

My uncle got this incredible smile on his face. Much to my surprise, he announced to the congregation that I had come forward to give my life to the preaching of the gospel. He put me into a small, side room to think about this great decision. And all I could think was, "What am I doing here?"

The following Sunday, my three friends and I were baptized by my uncle. Once more, he announced to the assembled congregation that I had given myself over to the Lord to preach.

If only he had asked me. That wasn't what I intended at all. I was twelve—more interested in records than religion. I attended Sunday school fairly regularly over the next few years. I wasn't committed and the thought of preaching was far from my mind.

High school changed me as I guess it does most of us. I began to grow up. I met the girl that I would later marry and began to think longer term. That's when I began to get serious about the church and religion. OK, not just church, but *her* church. I wasn't going with my family. I was attending with hers. Dad didn't go to church that much. He managed to make it about three times each year. So we were just dropped off at church each Sunday.

High school was a time for learning for me, not just in class, but in church, too. Her preacher and her parents were only too happy to oblige me. High school was a catalyst for my faith. Anne's parents were especially kind and I still regard them with as much love as I do my own. Together, they taught me that being a Christian was a lot more than just professing one's faith. It meant dedicating your life to the teachings of Jesus and living as He would have you live.

That was a revelation to me. It wasn't just memorizing Bible passages and going to church. It was living the word of God. My life began to change over-night. Even my friends and teammates at school noticed a difference.

I learned fairly quickly after graduation that I wasn't cut out to major in Petroleum Engineering at Texas Tech. I think most Texans consider the oil industry because it's so dominant in our state. But you have to love it and I didn't.

It didn't take long before I found myself called to the ministry. While at Tech, I met some very good people at the Bible Chair, which was supported by the Broadway Church of Christ. I became a regular at the Chair, attending devotionals and even signing up for my first Bible Course. (It was still recognized as an elective. I'm not sure you can take anything like that at state schools now. Too politically incorrect.)

That was the beginning of a great awakening in me. I was becoming a serious student of the Bible. It was when I went home for a semester that I began to realize my uncle had been partially right. I had always been drawn to the idea of working in the ministry in some capacity, but really didn't feel "called to preach." My calling led me to Abilene Christian where I could get the education in the Bible that I needed to answer that call. (It didn't hurt that my high school sweetheart was going to be there.)

My life's course took a sharp turn for the better.

Abilene Christian helped me grow into the man of faith I am today. Going to college in the place I was born turned into a rebirth for me. My work in the local church became a basis for all that I was doing at the time. I spent the next three years pouring myself into the studies I had chosen. I didn't stop for summer break. I kept on plugging away.

At the end of my senior year, I was even one of the five students selected to present their senior sermon at one of the local churches. I found myself standing at the pulpit of the college church with most of my professors sitting on the first two rows, preaching a sermon I am sure that all of them had heard many times before.

It was a packed house and it reminded me of that revival meeting where my uncle said I was chosen to preach. He was getting his wish or maybe he really knew, I couldn't tell. But even though I had performed in front of crowds hundreds of times before, I was nervous. This wasn't music. This didn't come easily to me. It was about faith.

It wasn't my best presentation, but I survived. I barely remember what I even talked about and I doubt any in the church do either. I crammed a thirty-minute sermon into fourteen minutes. I talked so fast that I may have broken the sound barrier at one point.

Yet, somehow, my professors still saw something in me. The next year, I attended graduate school and in 1965, I found myself working as the Educational Director and Youth Minister for a church in Odessa.

Those five years I worked actively in the ministry were probably some of the most difficult jobs in the world. Serving as a youth minister is like herding cats—except cats don't drive, get drunk, get pregnant, get arrested and a host of other things that young people do while they are learning to walk their way in this life.

Ministers are on call 24-7, but the youth minister gets a lot of calls when kids want to avoid telling their parents. It's got a high burnout factor. Sure, I loved every one of those young people and I was glad to help them. It just wasn't how I saw my life. And youth pastors either move up to becoming full pastors or they tend to move on. Moving on was a better move for me.

Not how I envisioned my life, but God has a way of taking our plans and turning them into His own. I tried a full-time career in faith—first in churches and then in academia. My "planned career" didn't work out. I think now that I was trying too hard. I wanted so much to live my faith that I forgot what I had learned in high school. That you don't have to be a minister to live a Christian life and to lead others in that life.

Leaving the full-time ministry in 1971 didn't mean I had left the ministry. I found myself still wanting to offer my education and experience to the local church where I was a member. I had a difficult time figuring out how to do that for a few years.

Once again, my marriage to Susan helped set me on the right path in my life. After our wedding, I set about getting my life in order. I began to work as a volunteer youth minister for our local Midland church and even taught a Sunday school class. And then there was music. Music is one of the ways I love to express my faith. I was a natural to serve as the Sunday morning song leader for our worship services.

That's become one of my roles in church. Since that time, I have filled those positions at the congregations where we have worshipped. Currently, I teach the senior class at the Fairmont Park Church of Christ in Midland, a non-denominational congregation.

My Sunday school usually has fifty to sixty attendees, and my own personal stool. If you read in the scriptures, they often say that Jesus sat down to teach. He did so in the temple. He sat in the boat when teaching to the crowd at Galilee. So I bought myself my own stool and I sit down to teach as well.

Our church is amazing because it's more than a building, it's a community of faith. A good-sized one. We fill the church with 700 people on a typical Sunday morning. We don't have any instrumental music there, no piano, no orchestra like some churches. So we just do vocals. Lots of singing. And singing is always one of the high points of any service for me.

We remodeled everything about five years ago. New facilities, new sound system and a better way to serve our community and spread the gospel. It was a $5-million project. I hosted the fundraising dinner and we invited fifty families to it. We raised $1.8 million in pledges that very night.

The church elders recently approached me to act as a fill-in preacher for area churches when they need a Sunday replacement for either a song leader, Sunday school teacher or someone to preach for them.

Once more, my uncle gets his wish.

I am actually able to use the education that I received at Abilene Christian and still pursue my career in the financial services industry. I find that, in a lot of ways, there is not too much difference from the way I helped people then to the way I help them now.

I am filling a void in the lives of my clients that offers them financial peace of mind. Sometimes, while visiting with them, I occasionally find myself assisting them with a family crisis or a spiritual need.

To help others, you need to help yourself. You need to keep your own soul at peace. I think spirituality is like a glass. You have to refill it constantly so you can pour it out to help others. One of the ways I do that starts with this little book that stays on my desk every day.

It was given to me by one of my clients. It has a different prayer and message each day. This is my everyday thing when I come in the morning. I look at the date on my phone and pick up the book and read. There's always something that's meaningful and it helps center me to start the work day.

Managing time is an important part of that. We get so caught up in our work day that we forget to include our faith. We get these twenty-four segments of time each day. We set aside eight for sleep (on a good day), another eight or more for work. Throw in a couple for eating and another one or two for commuting. Before you know it, your day is gone.

If you don't set aside time every day for your faith, it ends up being an afterthought. God gives us an amount of time on this earth to do the things we are supposed to accomplish. When our time is done, I don't think we'll care much if we made every meeting on time or got to work fifteen minutes early. But we'll care about how we treated others and we'll care if we set aside time to be the people God intended.

That, to me, is what faith is all about. It's not just attending church on Sunday and being miserable the rest of the week—to yourself and others. It's living your faith, being kind to others and trying even in our own small ways to be the people Jesus expected us to be.

That's why religion is the centerpiece for my life.

DEE'S DIRECTIVES:

You Don't Have To Retire, You Do Have To Plan To Do So.

I'm a planner. That kind of personality fits well with my job. Most Americans aren't. We're a spontaneous society. Have a whim? Follow the Nike motto: "Just do it!"

That can work fine if you are deciding whether to go to the movies or cook up some BBQ on the grill. It doesn't work fine when you get to long-term financial planning. And, sooner or later, we all need to get into long-term financial planning. You need to listen up even if you aren't a planner like me.

God willing, one day you're going to hit retirement age. That doesn't mean you have to retire then, but it would sure be nice to have the option. Wouldn't it? I'm already past retirement age. My wife Susan and I have saved for many years, so I know we could retire if we wanted to do so. We have the option. I just haven't exercised it.

I know, you aren't ready to retire just yet. The problem is, you might be 20, 30 or even 40 years from that date. The idea of retirement might be as foreign to you as living on Mars. Maybe more so. Americans drive the rest of the world crazy with our Protestant work ethic and our long hours. Our work helps define who we are. That makes it difficult to envision being retired.

You might be, like me and never truly plan to retire. Or, you might change your mind when that date gets closer. And if you didn't have a financial plan, that decision will be made for you. Imagine waking up on your 67th or 70th birthday and wanting to tell work you just quit—only you don't have enough money to get past the end of the month. Those dreams of golden years go flying out the window and you end up trying to buy Ramen Noodles at the store on sale like someone just out of school.

The news is filled with stories of people just like that. Career men and women in their 70s who have to work just to put food on the table. Me, I choose to work, I don't have to do so. That's why you need to plan for retirement. You want to have that choice.

There's more than just you at stake. You might be married and you certainly want to ensure your spouse has no financial worries. Then there's the children. You want to care for them. And you certainly don't want to dump your financial problems on them. It would be irresponsible.

Then there's the good stuff to plan to do. Retirement is a second act. It gives you the chance to travel that work and parenting never gave you. It lets you take up hobbies or treat yourself because you have the spare time to enjoy life.

But enjoying life takes more than time. It takes money. And that takes planning ahead.

Dee and Family taken in Germany late 1945 early 1946

Dee's Dad with his NCO and fellow officer's, conference room The Eagle's Nest 1945

Dee at Abilene Christian University Officials Locker Room

Dee as a Elvis Tribute Artist

11.

Fair to Midland

THERE ARE BIG REASONS why I love West Texas. I was born here. I grew up here and, except for a little time in California, I've lived here all my life. And that's only the beginning.

Texas is an enormous state and it's unfair to say any part of it defines Texas. I'm sure the city folk in Dallas and Houston would claim they do, for example. But what the rest of the country thinks of as Texas is right here in Midland-Odessa. My customers come from both places.

The two cities are sister communities, just a few miles down Interstate-20 from one another. We are smack dab in the Permian Basin,[43] an area that includes West Texas and southeast New Mexico. The name means we have lots of rocks from the Permian geological period. What that means in Texas terms is simple.

Oil.

And natural gas, too. Midland County has the second-highest number of drilling rigs in the basin and the highest is just down the road in Reeves County, according to one of the industry publications.

That means everywhere I drive around both cities, there are pump jacks, rocking back and forth pulling oil out of the ground, all hooked up to pipelines. There are even two on a golf course at the local country club. A golf course with pump jacks is almost stereotypical Texas.

Everything outside the cities is sort of a desert tan except the jacks. They're all painted the different colors of the companies that own them, which helps make it easy for maintenance workers to get the right ones. Two of my nephews are involved in that kind of work. They travel to a well, check the jack to make sure it's pumping correctly, finish and move on to the next one. It's a job that has to be done before the heat of the day. They get up at 3 a.m. and are home by noon.

We don't have a lot of rain in West Texas. Instead of water, we have oil. It's a fair trade. When oil is over $100, the area looks like Times Square on New Year's Eve, filled with people desperate to get the oil out of the ground as fast as possible. But even when the oil price drops, the infrastructure is still there. People keep working, just not as many.

Oil men and women make up much of the community. Several of the tall buildings in Midland have oil companies in them and have for decades. There's a beautiful twelve-story building downtown called the Petroleum Building[44] (used to be named for oilman T.S. Hogan). It was built in 1928, if that gives you an idea of oil's hold on our local economy.

Restaurants, financial services (like me), realtors and even churches count on them. They're hard-working, independent, incredible people. They might be rich one minute and poor the next, but they aren't the stereotypes Hollywood has created. I don't know any J.R. Ewings.

They are tough, ideal successors to the cowboys who made West Texas famous in movies. When people cite the Texas slogan, "Don't Mess With Texas," they are the kind of people you don't want to mess with. But they will give you the shirt off their backs if you are in need and go to store and get you shoes to match.

That toughness comes through in everything West Texas is known for, especially sports. If you've seen "Friday Night Lights" or read H.G. Bissinger's book "Friday Night Lights: A Town, a Team, and a

Dream,"[45] you know something of West Texas. The novel was based on Odessa's Permian High School Panthers as they try to win a championship.

West Texans love our sports—not usually the big-league kind, either. We like high school sports because those are about our community. We go see our sons (and sometimes our daughters) catch the winning touchdown or shoot the winning basket. Sports are about our families and our community.

They bring all of us closer.

Sports have always been a part of my life. I played pick-up games as a child and then moved on to organized teams because, again, this is West Texas. We do youth sports like we do oil. Both are big, messy and drilled down deep into who we are.

There are lots of ways to get involved as I found out one college afternoon. I was playing three-on-three basketball with five friends who were going to graduate school with us. "Shorty" Lawson, the assistant superintendent for athletics from Abilene schools, came walking into the gym. He was another Abilene Christian alumnus and we all knew him.

Shorty was a legend and still is, though he passed away in 2010. He gave his whole life to athletics to helping form young minds by teaching them sports. But he was also a legend in officiating. He refereed basketball and football for more than thirty years at the highest level -- Cotton Bowl games, Fiesta Bowl Games, the Sugar Bowl, the Orange Bowl. You name it, he refereed it. And when he wasn't refereeing the games, he was teaching others to do so.

We stop the game and Shorty walks up to us and ask, "Would any of you guys like to referee basketball?" We all laughed and looked at him like he had lost his mind. Who wants to be a referee? In sports, one team gets to win. The ref always loses.

Shorty had heard that response before and had the perfect one to throw back at us. "We pay cash and you can do as many games as you want." I stopped laughing and started paying closer attention. He said we could do almost ten games a week if we wanted and it was $10 a game.

I was earning just $55 a week for loading boxes four hours a day. I was making $2.50 an hour and breaking my back doing it. They played three games a day, three days a week. So I could do nine hours work and get a huge raise in the process. Of course, there was prep work involved but it was still a lot more money and a lot more fun.

I started refereeing soon after, while I was still in graduate school. One of my professors was also a basketball official. He loaned me my first striped shirt and gave me a whistle. I started officiating then and it lasted till 1997—more than thirty years.

The only break I took was when I lived in California. They tried to get me to ref there, but the game was a different game than the one they played in Texas. I was a Division I official and I figured I'd check out a game. And it was filled with technical fouls and the crowd was rowdier than I liked. So I passed.

That plaque I mentioned that Abilene Christian put up honoring my service was tied in to my years of refereeing. It is on the wall outside the officials' dressing room in the new Wildcat Stadium and says those facilities were provided by Dee Carter, class of '64.

You'd be amazed at the number of people you meet refereeing youth and college sports. Thousands. Athletes, coaches, parents and fans all get to know the regular refs. If you're good, they grow to respect you. Not necessarily like, that's for off-court. On the court, the best a referee can hope for is respect. And you're only one real bad call away from losing that.

I don't have too many bad stories from refereeing and it sure seemed like both the children and the school administrators liked me. Even the coaches, though they couldn't admit it. But I was out one night refereeing a game between Midland and Midland Lee and I realized that no matter what happened, half the people in town would be mad at me. And some of them were bound to be my clients.

Once I thought it through, I stopped calling local games. It seemed a good business decision and I like going to the store and not running into someone who's mad at me.

No matter how hard you try, weird conflicts happen. There was a basketball tournament at Abilene Christian one time and I was scheduled to referee. The games are picked at random and I saw I was refereeing Abilene Christian vs. Southwest Texas State University (now, Texas State).

It got even more complicated. I noticed my high school basketball coach in the stands. I went and said hi and asked why he was there. His son was coaching Texas State. I remembered him when he was a three-year-old.

He grew up—enough to win that night and he looked me up after the game. He said his Dad had mentioned how he coached me and he remembered me as well. He thanked me for refereeing a fair game but admitted he didn't know I had gone to Abilene Christian until after it was over. "I would have been sweating bullets," he told me, if he had known. That was more my experience—being treated professionally.

I kept close ties to the high school in Monahans, where I had gone. I refereed there and ran their basketball tournament for a number of years. Back in 1993, I was considering retiring from officiating, though I got talked out of it later. One day I was at Monahans, getting ready to referee the finals that night and one of the students came into the dressing room and said they needed me out on the court to sort out a problem.

I didn't even have my striped shirt on yet. So I just zipped up my jacket and went out to find what mess I had to cope with. The team was all on the court and the media was there waiting for me. The players had taken up a collection and presented me with a beautiful engraved plaque and gave it to me as thanks.

That's the only memento that I keep from my refereeing days and I do so because it was given to me by the players. That's who the game is all about.

I'm not always a referee, though it sometimes seems like it. We've been season ticket holders for football teams here in Midland. We try to go to as many games as we can. We can't go to all of them, but we try.

I used to be a season ticket holder for our baseball team—the AA RockHounds[46]—but got too busy. The team is part of the Oakland A's system and have been winning like the Yankees. They've won Texas League championships in the last four years.

Minor league games give you a first look at talent before they arrive on the national scene. I've seen stars like Joe Carter,[47] Jim Edmonds[48] and Barry Zito[49] refine their game before heading on the big leagues. Shawon Dunston[50] who was the first draft pick of the Chicago Cubs in 1982 played here. He was good but he hated to walk. He wanted to hit the ball. I always respected that, but he would have had an even-better career if he learned to take a pitch.

If you imagine the movie "Bull Durham," it's much the same thing. A lot of players trying hard to make the big leagues and only a few ever do. But we love them.

The best part of minor league baseball is you get to know the players really well. That's what happens in a small market. The players go to the homes of the fans and have dinner—in large part because they are paid so little that they can barely afford to eat.

One time I was in San Antonio conducting some business, and I found out that Midland was playing San Antonio that night. I figured it was a great chance to see the team, and minor league games seldom sell out, so a good ticket was easy to find.

I went that evening to the game and I asked for a ticket near the Midland dugout. The ticket lady said she could put me right next to it. I lucked out and they just happened to announce that Sandy Koufax was signing autographs that very night. Talk about luck! When they did, I leaned down into the dugout and said to manager, "Skip, give me a ball." He recognized me and I think he was glad to have at least one fan for an away game, so he tossed me one.

I go and get in line and it's a couple dozen little children and me. I doubt if they knew who Koufax[51] was, but he's signing these baseballs, left-handed of course, and he gets to me and stares. He looks me up and down and says, "Are you going to sell this?" There's such a market for memorabilia, I couldn't blame him for being skeptical.

I shook my head and responded, "No sir. I used to lay awake at night listening to you pitch when the Dodgers were the Brooklyn

Dodgers. I've wanted your autograph ever since." I told him how I tried to pitch in high school but it just wasn't in me. I could see a smile go across his face. It looked just for a second like he was back on the mound again and the years seemed to disappear.

He signed it and it has a place of honor in my office. So I've got a Texas League ball signed by Sandy Koufax. There can't be that many of those around. It sits right near a ball signed by another amazing pitcher, Nolan Ryan.[52]

There's a lot more to West Texas than sports. Midland features a star-quality performing arts center, part of the University of Texas of the Permian Basin in Odessa—or UTPB because that's a mouthful. It's officially the Wagner Noël Performing Arts Center[53] and seats up to 1,800 people. It's such an awesome facility that it draws the top acts—people like Jerry Seinfeld and Clint Black.

I'll admit it's my favorite building on the outside—too modern. But on the inside it's beautiful. It's built in the same style as Carnegie Hall with lots of air for the sound to travel. I'm out there eight, ten times a year. Our chorale group performs there and every Tuesday night we're out by the airport practicing.

I'm incredibly proud of The Midland-Odessa Symphony & Chorale and I have a right to be. It's the quality of what a city twice our size or more might have and it's been going strong for 55 years. We employ seventy professional musicians and the chorale has eighty singers, including me. I'm also on the board of directors with some wonderful people.

We have an unusual event scheduled where they'll show the movie "The Wizard of Oz." The orchestra will play the music and the chorale will sing some of the songs as well. I even had the honor of conducting the final number for the Midland-Odessa Symphony Christmas concert one year. I've got my own baton now.

It was one of the few times in my career where I pointed at people and they did exactly what I asked. I think every employer should have one.

Oil, sports and music might sound like they mix as poorly as oil and water. In West Texas, they are key ingredients to our community.

Your community has different things that are important to it, different ideas and ideals. It's still a community. The author John Donne wrote that, "No man is an island." That includes you and me. We need to get out, get to know our neighbors and become part of our community.

You'll be better for it.

DEE'S DIRECTIVES:

You Are Aging Like Fine Wine.

"You're not getting older, you're getting better." That was an advertising slogan for hair dye back in the 1970s. It was around the time that marketers started realizing that older people spent money, too. So they geared products and even the occasional TV show to an older audience. ("Golden Girls" wasn't designed with teens in mind.)

It's time to own up to it. You're not as young as you used to be. Don't hide from it. Own it. So I want you plan like I discussed in the last chapter. Only I want you to work on two types of plans, not one.

First, plan for you and your family. Plan to enjoy life during your retirement. This can't be just a casual effort. I want you to commit time to figuring it out—travel, hobbies, things you want to buy.

If you have a computer, create a file and put everything in a Word document. I want you to be systematic. Create categories for travel, hobbies, purchases and more. Whatever you think might entertain you in your retirement.

Take your time and be thorough. Be sure to include your spouse in this exercise. Go state by state in the U.S. and think about the places you've never seen. Haven't seen the Grand Canyon or Mt. Rushmore? Put them down. Or maybe you want to catch a show on

Broadway or take that cruise to Alaska. Foreign travel is just the same. Take a course with a famous chef or go swimming off a beach in Tahiti.

Then list expected expenses. Put some budget lines next to those trips and purchases. Factor in any expected big-ticket items—children's college, weddings, home repairs and anything else. Do you plan to downsize? Perhaps you want to move to a warmer or friendlier tax climate.

Now you need to overlay the dates that are significant. I explained earlier that age 50 starts giving you a chance to catch up financially. Here are a few other key milestones. This is just the shorthand version to get you thinking. Work with your financial advisor for more detail. These tips come to you from your government—a mix of the IRS and the Social Security Administration.[54]

55—If you lose your job, you can take money from your employer-sponsored retirement plan without penalty.

59½—There's no penalty to withdraw from the employer-sponsored retirement plans but you still have to pay taxes.

62—This is the age where you can start receiving partial Social Security retirement benefits. If you were born before 1960, the date when you can collect full benefits varies a bit.

65—When most Americans become eligible for Medicare.

67—The point where you are eligible for full Social Security benefits.

70—The point where you are eligible for maximum Social Security benefits.

70½—Required Minimum Distributions must begin by this age.

That's hardly complete. No list will be. It's intended to get you started and so you understand just how complex retirement can be. There's a lot you should want to do. And a lot of dates you need to work around to do it.

12.

Some Gave All

WEST TEXAS HAS DEEP ties to the military, Midland, especially. Just as I do. The airport used to be known first as Sloan Field[55] and then became the top bombardier training center during World War II. It's now called Midland International Air & Space Port.

That's no joke. Midland was the first commercial space port in the U.S. It's a big draw to get R&D firms to locate in the area. And it adds to the excitement about flight.

There's an annual celebration every Memorial Day involving reconditioned old planes run by the Commemorative Air Force.[56] (It used to be the Confederate Air Force but that's not politically correct now.)

I grew up loving the military. That's only natural when you see your dad serving, all decked out in his dress uniform. Boys used to all dream of the adventure of war. Soldiers, sailors and airmen know it's hard, dangerous and deadly. But they do it anyway because it has to be done. They are proud to serve their country, proud to risk everything so we can be free.

My Dad was in the Army for sixteen years and only resigned his commission after I was already in college. Dad's serial number is

01336876. I saw it on so many footlockers, I know it by heart. I don't think I ever knew what that phrase meant until I just wrote those words. "By heart." Yes, that's exactly how I remember so much about Dad and that number reminds me of him.

Thanks to Dad, the military has always been part of my life. We lived in a half dozen military bases. I wanted to follow in his footsteps and that meant signing up for Air Force ROTC.

ROTC was a big part of my life for two years. We'd march and train and learn the military way of doing everything. I still walk straight like they taught me fifty-plus years ago. If you did well, every six weeks they'd take one of us on a flight. This was the Air Force and they wanted to see if they had any potential pilots. It was also one heck of an incentive for ROTC cadets to work hard.

This was what I thought I wanted to do, so I signed up for it. When I got my chance to fly in a jet, it was incredible how fast we went. The pilot was doing maybe 550 or 600 miles per hours and you watched the world race by—roads, towns, even cities. He took us down toward Dallas and then near Austin and back and the whole trip took us only a little more than an hour and ten minutes. All over the whole state of Texas in a short space of time.

We were on our way back to what used to be Reese Air Force Base,[57] west of Lubbock. Then he let me take control. Boy, that was an unbelievable thrill, the biggest thrill in the world, I thought. You barely touched the stick and the plane would react instantly, just heel over and go. It's like the two of you are merged together. I've done a bunch of horseback riding. This was different. A horse might react to how you guide it, but slowly. This was instantaneous.

He talked to me through the headset and asked me if I was up to doing some rolls. I didn't hesitate, I was having too much fun. "Go for it!" I hollered back. He took over again and rolled the plane over so we were flying upside down. We're flying facing the ground at 25,000 feet going maybe 600 mph.

What a rush!

I'm running out of words to describe how cool it was. Then he hit me with a barrel roll, sending the jet spinning out to the right. Next he looped us up and over, showing the power of the plane beneath me.

When we touched ground, the pilot congratulated me. He said most people "lose their cookies" on some of those maneuvers. I didn't. I loved it and wanted to go back. So I worked real hard and earned a chance to go back up. I'll never forget it. Or the men I knew who served.

I lost two of my classmates from Abilene Christian in Vietnam. They were pilots, too. Their names on are on the Vietnam War Memorial in Washington. It's a fitting tribute, but not enough. They're another reason why I do the Honor Flights.

My call to the ministry was the direction my life took, but it didn't change the love and respect I have for the guys in uniform. I've always felt like I missed the boat because I didn't serve. But by the time I got my draft notice in 1963, I had wrecked my knee playing basketball and I couldn't go. They wouldn't take me on a dare.

Lots of my friends and clients have served in the military. Helping the flights has allowed me to help them, to pay them back.

My best friend Buck was a Huey helicopter pilot in Vietnam before he went into the insurance business. He racked up 1,400 hours in one of those birds. That was two tours. He had one shot down and he lived to tell the tale. Another copter's engines blew out on takeoff and he pancaked back down. Wasn't his fault and he was lucky to survive once again.

Year before last, he went back to Fort Bragg[58] because they recognized his unit as the No. 1 rescue unit from the war. The air rescue services were credited overall with saving more than 4,000 lives during the war. He's still mighty proud of the work he did.

One man came up to him at Bragg and said, "I've got to meet you." It was a retired general and he thanked Buck for saving so many of his men during the war. Buck said that was the best "Thank you" he ever got. When a general thanks you, it matters.

Buck never flew a helicopter again. He used to joke that they had all the maneuverability of a brick. He and his crew used to disengage the rotor and drop like one of those bricks to get into a hot landing zone and then turn the engine back on at the last possible second. It was risky but it worked.

One of my clients was in Vietnam and dropped off in a hot zone doing exactly that. Maybe even by Buck himself. They're both who the Honor Flights are designed for.

Every American above a certain age knows where they were on 9/11. It defined a generation like Pearl Harbor had sixty years before. It's another reason why so many of us in Midland help the Honor Flight.

I was in Salt Lake City, Utah at a national convention when 9/11 happened. I was past president of the National Association of Insurance and Financial Advisors-Texas.

They immediately canceled the convention. I learned that one of my friends at the convention couldn't get hold of his son. He worked in the tower. A group of about ten of us were close and we stayed with him the whole time as he tried to reach his son. We cried and prayed together all day long. He's Jewish and I'm Christian and it didn't matter. All of us were there for him.

Finally, about 5 p.m., almost eight hours after the attacks, he heard from his son. He had made it out alive. I don't know if I've ever felt anything like that—the sense of relief. It was like a giant weight had been lifted off my soul.

We went to a special patriotic prayer service at the Mormon Temple that night and the Mormon Tabernacle Choir sang. It was so moving that it brought a lot of the audience to tears.

We were all trapped in Las Vegas, trying to get home with no flights out. The only way to get home was to rent a van to get back to Texas. I called the rental car people and they weren't optimistic. Finally, two days later, they found us a van and six of us headed home together in a giant road trip, almost 1,000 miles.

Eventually, we got home. Back to our normal lives. But back East, we knew there were thousands of families who were struggling with what happened. We also knew that it meant more war. That the men and women in the military would have to answer the call.

The flights are for them.

We had our first opportunity with the Honor Flights in Midland in 2014. There were two guys in my Sunday school senior group class who were WWII veterans. I wanted to thank them, so I sponsored them on the first Honor Flight. And I went as the guardian for one of them.

That led me to the Honor Flight meetings, where one of the men there recognized me because of my radio show on KWEL. He told me I could be a big part of what they do. They wanted my help doing commercials and working with them on media. I wasn't about to refuse. The next I thing I knew, I was a volunteer and a board member.

It didn't stop there. The Honor Flight is top-notch group and if you are willing to help, they will keep on giving you things to do. Soon, I was emceeing events, serving as a bus captain or even just unloading wheelchairs.

Then they hit me with the big one—singing the national anthem at Arlington National Cemetery. If that doesn't choke you up, you're dead from the heart up. It was one of the great honors of my life. That whole first flight tore my heart out.

Taking a couple dozen veterans to Washington, DC. requires all the coordination of a military operation. If you ever go, take plenty of Kleenex because every stop along the way, might make you cry.

Let me tell you what just one visit was like. Because the Honor Flight isn't about me. It's about the veterans. This is their story.

We took off from Midland in 2015 but we were met at the airport by an honor guard of local emergency services personnel—police, sheriff's office and fire department, complete with flags. It was quite moving for both the veterans and the volunteers.

We shared some gift packages for them to read on the plane. They were prepared by local school children and included "Thank you" notes and letters telling about the military men and women in their own families. Each of the veterans had several to read and I saw them passing them around, eager to share the good feelings.

We landed at Baltimore-Washington International, north of D.C. and were met by our local contacts. But what was inspiring was the reaction of the other travelers. They started applauding and cheering when they realized who we were. Men and women, young and old of all races. I wanted to hug every one of them.

They kept on clapping, some even coming up to the veterans and shaking their hands. More thanks, even a few hugs and kisses. It was a Texas-sized welcome and I know they appreciated it.

The next day we took them into the heart of D.C. to see the many monuments there—Vietnam, Korea, World War II and more. Each of those has its own character, its own grandeur.

The World War II Memorial has a majesty all its own. It features 56 pillars and arches that honor people from all the different states that served. There's a Freedom Wall of stars facing the Reflecting Pool with more than 4,000 stars, each representing 100 Americans who died in the war.

We held a ceremonial wreath laying at the memorial, complete with bagpiper Clint Adams and an honor guard, who followed us around to each monument. Everywhere we went, the visitors joined in once more, applauding and cheering our veterans. We had one WWII veteran with us who was 100-years-old—Manuel Herrera. We were honored to get him to see the memorial that he helped build with his bravery. He's what the Honor Flights are all about.

The tour took them to the Korean Memorial next. Where the WWII Memorial is grandiose, the Korean monument is understated. It features a small unit of soldiers moving through the grass as if out on patrol. We saw it in the bright sun of a summer's day, but I've seen photos of it enshrouded in fog or covered by snow where it looks life-like.

We escorted the veterans over to the Vietnam Memorial, done in a completely different style. The Vietnam Memorial took the personal touch. Everyone who died in that awful conflict is on the wall. Mr. Herrera's son Ben was killed in Vietnam and it must have brought back some good memories and some tough ones to see his name there.

The tour also stopped at the Lincoln Memorial and the Smithsonian Air & Space Museum. I think those stops lightened the load on the veterans and guides alike. It was a day both inspiring and emotionally draining.

And we weren't done.

The Honor Flight culminated with a trip to Arlington Cemetery. It's a solemn event. The bus is usually escorted by a police car to the cemetery. Not a word was spoken as it drove in. All you heard was the drone of the heavy engine. The veterans were lost in thought, remembering both their own time at war and those friends they lost, many who were buried right there.

As we escorted them off the bus, the first thing that struck us was the beauty of the place. There were flowers everywhere and their fragrance added to the peace of the moment. Our flight was part of a formal wreath-laying ceremony at the Tomb of The Unknown Soldier.[59] Everything about that—the changing of the guard, the symbolic laying of the wreath, was done with respect and precision. It's as if any misstep would be disrespecting the dead. So there were no missteps.

From there we moved to Section 60, a newer section devoted to those killed in our nation's most recent wars—Iraq and Afghanistan. Our Chairman John West lost his son Matthew in Afghanistan and he was buried in Section 60. We helped him lay a wreath at Matthew's grave. We had three families with sons buried there. So it was a very emotional moment. They asked me to do the prayer and I had nothing prepared. So I went back in the bus and prayed for guidance, prayed for the right words. I don't know what I ended up saying, I just turned it over to the Lord. And it must have worked because everyone was very moved.

I'll be honest, I don't remember a word of what I said.

I have stayed involved in the Honor Flight in memory of my Dad who died way too young, not even 68 when he had his second stroke. Those efforts are a tribute to what he did in his years with the Army. It goes back to something I wrote in the first chapter. Even now, older than my Dad was when he passed and I'm still out there to make him proud.

We've made five flights—every one of them both a memory for me and for the veterans who fly with us. Funny thing is, I'm older than some of the vets who go on the trips, but they don't know that. I'm going to keep on helping out, though I had to drop my spot on the board to work on this book.

The Honor Flights give all of us a chance to give the respect due to those who ensured we have so much. It's one of the best things I've ever been involved with.

DEE'S DIRECTIVES:

The Government Wants You To Catch Up.

You might remember the fable of the ant and the grasshopper. The ant was a hardworking sort. He'd labor long days to store up food for the winter. The grasshopper was a happy-go-lucky fellow who carried a violin under his arm. He made music day and night, living the party life.

Then winter came. The ant had plenty to eat and a warm shelter because he had planned ahead. The grasshopper was left out in the cold to starve. The fable, attributed to Aesop but told in various ways, was hardly subtle. It takes work to plan for winter. You can party all you want, but you'll suffer later.

We all know people who are like the grasshopper. They want the nicest new cars and the fanciest clothes. They go only to the best restaurants and you wonder how they can manage the vacations they take. I know a lot of "ants" in my business, too. They plan for the future.

I help both personalities. So does Uncle Sam. Various tax breaks add retirement saving. But there are special set-asides once you hit 50 so you can make up for lost ground.

If you have access to a 401(k), the standard limit on deposits is $18,000 a year, according to our friends at the IRS. That sounds like a lot, only few people max out their contributions. And do that only when they get older. Once you hit your 50th year, that limit goes up to $24,500 a year. (Your employer may set a lower limit.)

The same happens with traditional or Roth IRAs. Both have a standard $5,500 limit per year. That jumps to $6,500 per year after you hit 50. Unfortunately, the tax benefits for the 401(k) plans and the IRAs conflict.

The tax benefits can be curtailed if you have a retirement plan at work. Single filers or heads of households can earn up to $62,000 adjusted gross income and have no problems. The benefit is limited from $62,000 to $72,000. Above that, there is no tax benefit according to IRS rules.[60]

Those numbers go up for married couples filing jointly or for widowed taxpayers. You can probably tell that this starts to get complicated. Then there's the most obvious way to catch up—become the most enterprising ant you have ever seen. That means save, save and save some more. This has to be a two-fold strategy—cutting spending and saving. Just one side of that won't work.

First you have to go back to your budget and examine it with a fine-tooth comb. Cut everything you don't need—slice that cable bill and hack your entertainment expenses. Skip meals out and pack that lunch. If you can take mass transit instead of driving, do it if it's cheaper. Analyze every spending category and look at how it can be cut.

The reverse goes on savings. Max out any and all approved retirement plans and IRAs for starters. Then keep saving every bit you can. If that doesn't get you on the path you need, consider taking on a part-time job. Then save all that money, too.

Yes, this is a lot easier if you have a professional assist you figuring out all of these moves.

13.

God Bless
The USA (politics)

I DON'T HIDE MY POLITICS. Being a conservative in West Texas is like being an oil jack, there's one in whichever direction you look. You don't have to agree with me. In fact, you have a right to disagree.

That's what freedom is all about.

I know, it doesn't seem anyone thinks like that anymore. Too many voices on the left and right want to silence the other side. Students who want to support the president get silenced or bullied on college campuses. Social media companies use their power to silence those that they disagree with. And other powerful tech companies like Google do the same.

I do a radio show every week on KWEL. I can't imagine being told that I can't or that there are political positions I can't state on air. No matter what political side you claim to be on, this debate should be worrisome.

Strangely, it's not. As much as politics has invaded every aspect of our lives, this fight hasn't. Part of it is too many younger people have been raised that it's a crime to offend them. They're even offended by the term "snowflake" that has been used to describe them.

That's only one of many things our younger generation gets dangerously wrong. According to one recent survey, forty-four percent of all millennials would prefer to live in a socialist system over a capitalist one.

They probably figured that out while drinking a Caramel Brulée Latte and checking Facebook on their iPhones—all three products of that marvelous capitalist system their young minds would oppose.

Everything in life now is politics it seems. And so much of it is wrong. We are still one nation. We have our disagreements, but like a smart businessman, I happily work with clients from all backgrounds. And I do my best to treat every one of them the best I can.

Most people know that both Bush presidents call Texas home. Few realize that it was Midland that housed the Bush family for four years during the early 1950s. George H. W. Bush bought a tiny rancher in 1951 for just $9,000. Even inflation doesn't make that into six figures sixty-six years later. He was frugal. I like that.

The house is now a museum, dedicated to two now-former presidents. Former Governor Jeb Bush, also lived there for a time. The home is an official Texas landmark, and is on the National Register of Historic Places. And the people in Midland still have great affection for both of their former presidents. I have a photo taken of me, President George W. Bush and Nolan Ryan that hangs on one wall of my office. I'm not in the habit of getting photos taken with presidents, so it's a nice keepsake. And a good hint to what I believe.

West Texas didn't start out this friendly to Republicans, that's for sure. Texas used to be a one-party state, just the other party from what it is now. In Texas, in the '50s and '60s, everyone was a Democrat. My Mom and Dad, even my grandparents, were all members of the Democrat Party and my Dad was actively involved with the election process when we lived in Monahans.

One hundred years ago, Midland was voting more than 91 percent for Democrats. Republicans got just 4 percent of the vote. Herbert Hoover changed that some, almost getting a majority of votes in the district. The GOP votes plummeted with the Great Depression, gradually rising as years passed.

I followed in my parents' footsteps and did my very first volunteer work in politics as a senior in high school as the political tide had already shifted right. I was young and idealistic and wanted to help the candidate for Congress from our district. I really enjoyed the work and we were successful in getting him elected to the office, though to be honest, I don't even recall his name now.

But leaving high school forced me to change in many ways. And my politics was part of that. I was an active supporter of John F. Kennedy, along with many young Democrats, even though I was too young to vote when he won in 1960. (Midland voted strongly against him.) His death in 1963, began to change my political philosophy. I began to notice that my views weren't always on track with the Democrat Party.

It didn't happen overnight.

JFK's successor as president was his vice president Lyndon Baines Johnson, LBJ we called him. He had been born in Stonewall, Texas, just north of San Antonio. LBJ spent twenty-four years in Congress from Texas—first as a congressman and then as senator. We knew him well and, let's just say, I didn't want any part of what he was selling.

The 1964 election settled things for me when he ran for a full term. I found myself being attracted to the conservative side of things and cast my very first presidential vote for Republican Barry Goldwater. He won handily in Midland with 57 percent of the vote. He was absolutely crushed nationally, losing 61.1 percent to 38.5 percent.

I tried not to talk about it too much with family. I thought my parents and grandparents were going to disown me. I weathered the storm, though I later learned one key reason. Dad had mysteriously seemed to support my choice. It turned out he had joined with the rest of the community and voted for Dwight Eisenhower for president in 1952. That was the beginning of a big shift in West Texas voting that lasts till today. Midland hasn't voted Democrat since. And Dad finally admitted publicly that he had shifted after he voted for Richard Nixon in 1968.

I didn't realize it at the time, but the realignment made a lot of sense. General Eisenhower had been Dad's commanding officer when he served in Germany in World War II. Ike had led a couple of million American men to defeat the Germans. It only made sense that many of them followed him when he ran for office and stuck with the GOP after he retired.

That was it for me. I was suddenly a full-fledged Republican and have been an active one in local, state and national elections since Goldwater. The local Republican Party even eyed me as a candidate for Congress several years ago. I quickly put the kibosh on that idea.

I supported the candidate, who happened to be a good friend of mine. But I never want to climb into the political arena for any office. I attend meetings, make phone calls and financially support the candidates of my choice, as I feel everyone should.

I'm not interested in running for any kind of elective office. There's a quote that relates to this from union General William Tecumseh Sherman.[61] "If nominated, I will not run; if elected, I will not serve." That works for me.

It just doesn't get to the heart of things that I believe.

"Walden" author Henry David Thoreau wrote in "Civil Disobedience" how he fully embraced the motto, "That government is best which governs least." He wanted to take it to extremes. I don't. But it makes a darn good Texas motto, even if I read it written by a man from Massachusetts.

My chief concerns in life revolve around liberty—the ability to be free in what you own, free in your right to believe in your faith and free in the right to defend those rights. Most everything else I support evolves from that.

National government is essential. Don't fall into the trap and think otherwise. It can fight wars to defend us, handle massive problems that cross state lines and deliver the kind of expertise local government can't afford.

The issue between left and right is simply how big does that government get?

It's too big already. And it's getting worse. It seems like no one in Washington is serious about cutting the deficit, much less the national debt. Our national debt[62] is over $20 trillion. And our national Gross Domestic Product (everything we make and build in the U.S.) was just $19.79 trillion[63] in February of 2018.

Put simply, we could tax every single thing that anybody made, build or invested in 2016 and it wouldn't pay off our debts. I know families can get in over their heads and it's hard and scary digging out. Imagine owing more on your credit cards than you earn in a year.

This isn't a family we're talking about. It's the greatest nation on earth and its debt to GDP ratio[64] is more than 104 percent. And there's no simple fix. We can't cut our government. The federal government is budgeted to spend a little more than $4.03 trillion in 2017. That means we have to shut down the government for five years to come close to paying it off.

Not going to happen.

We can't cut spending enough to deal with it. We can't tax enough to deal with it ever. And if we inflated the money supply enough, we'd be pushing around wheelbarrows full of cash like they did in 1930s Germany.

It would be fantastic if we could grow the economy that fast, but the U.S. economy grows[65] around three percent a year typically. That's not happening on the current path, though it pushed past that toward the end of 2017. That's not enough so something has to give.

Ideally, it's a mix of all four. Yes, we need to shrink government. And though I hate taxes, a serious plan would raise them some way or another. The same with inflating the money[66]. We can survive a little.

It's the growth part we can control. And we do that by giving businesses more control over what they do. We do it by giving them much less regulation on how they do business and let the market pick the winners and losers, not the government.

The same goes for ordinary taxpayers. If you want to boost the American economy, give the citizens enough liberty so that they can start businesses and live free. Small businesses are the backbone of this economy. Strangle them with too much paperwork and no one starts one or, if they do, they do it under the table.

My view of guns is based on the same view of liberty. It's also very much grounded in Texas history. We won our independence from Mexico by being armed. There's a famous Texas flag that dates back to our War of Independence. The Mexican army had been ordered to seize a cannon from the town of Gonzales[67]. The citizens there refused to give in and, instead, designed a flag that read: "Come and take it," just below an image of a star and, below that, a cannon.

The Texicans knew their history. That phrase harkened back to the Spartans, who gave a similar response when told to give up their arms. That phrase in Greek was "Molon Labe"[68] and meant "Come and take them."

Almost two hundred years after Texas independence and I see no reason to trust government, or anyone else, enough to give up my gun rights. I'm a lifetime member of the NRA. I know sometimes guns are misused, but that's usually people doing so illegally. The vast majority of legal gun owners obey the law. Taking away their rights to stop criminals only penalizes law-abiding citizens.

We should all take our constitutional rights more seriously or they might just be taken away.

When I get talking about the Constitution, I am reminded how much I love this country. I talk about West Texas because it's special to me, a tiny piece of dusty paradise. But I get all choked up when I talk about America.

I spent years of my life putting on Elvis gear and entertaining. That was all a lot of fun. But when I'd sing "An American Trilogy," with its mixture of songs from our heritage, I'd see how inspired the crowd would get. And it inspired me.

We all get that feeling when we sing the national anthem. It stirs our hearts and our souls. It's the same feeling when we say the "Pledge of Allegiance" or maybe just when we get together with our neighbors for a barbecue.

America is more than any one of us. Whether it's singing, praying, traveling or just doing business around this great country, I've always seen us for all of our promise, overcoming our problems and pulling together to go into the future.

That's the America I love. And the reason why it continues to exist is thanks to the good and great men and women of the U.S. military. I've already told you of my deep feelings for those who serve. They're a key foundation to us staying free.

The idea of freedom takes me to one of the last points about politics that I need to make. It's a very personal one. Maybe one of the most personal of this book. I believe with all my heart that human life is sacred.

All people, no matter whether born or unborn, contribute to our world. I watched my little sister-Kay live for 70 years and saw how much she taught all of us. The same goes for my incredible daughter Erin. Both of them have faced enormous challenges because of Down syndrome. Both still have lived essential, important lives.

There are those who teach that we shouldn't value such lives. That we are wise enough to choose who should live and who should die. I don't believe that. I don't believe I am wiser than God who has a right to be here on this earth.

Those are the things I stand for. That's a good idea of my politics. You might agree a hundred percent, fifty percent or even zero. That's what makes the world go 'round.

But politics isn't supposed to be war by other means. We are a republic. We need to discuss and debate, argue and even disagree. Then we need to come together to make our decisions, not pull apart to make decisions on our own.

That's been tried in America and it cost 750,000[69] lives. Let's not try it again.

DEE'S DIRECTIVES:

Count Social Security, But Don't Count On It.

Social Security is an essential part of your retirement. It was created as a supplement to retirement savings. It's not supposed to provide enough money to live on comfortably. How much you get each month depends on how many years you work, how much money you make and our leaders in Washington, D.C.

That last one gets ignored in lots of money management debates. You see, entitlements—that's Medicare, Medicaid and Social Security—amount to future commitments of at least $74 trillion, according to the Milken Institute.[70] It will gradually get to a point where they eat up most of the federal budget.

As I write this, there is talk in Washington about "fixing" that problem. If you have already retired or are close to retiring, any fix probably won't impact you. If you are at least a few years away, you can expect some in the government might try and trim benefits as a way of keeping the debt from getting out of control.

The system is solvent for now and I wouldn't spend a lot of time worrying about it. But it's good to keep that in the back of your mind and focus on the major issues at hand.

Social Security calculates your payout based on 35 years of salary. If you are earning good money now, that might offset some low-earning years early in your career. Years where you earned nothing naturally count as zero.

As you saw in my last Dee's Directive, when you start collecting Social Security matters a great deal. There are actually three separate dates—when you initially qualify, when you qualify for full benefits and then when you qualify for maximum benefits.

Initial retirement is 62. Retire then and you will also receive the lowest of the three possible options. It might make sense if you need the income now or don't want to wait. That waiting only makes sense if it makes sense for you. Put off collecting Social Security until either full or maximum payout and you'll receive a lot more money each month—but for a shorter time period.

That ends up becoming a pretty complex calculus that, unfortunately, means you have to estimate how long you expect to receive it. Spousal benefits are also complicated and depend on when the other spouse started getting benefits.

You can see why you might want someone's advice to help you sort this out. Looking at it properly also forces us to contemplate our own mortality and few of us want to handle that task.

The best feature of Social Security is it won't run out. Were Methuselah alive today, he could collect his Social Security check for hundreds of years. That's why retiring early has significant consequences and can't be done lightly. The average retired worker receives a little more than $16,000 a year in benefits. That comes from figures at the Center on Budget and Policy Priorities.[71]

That's not enough to live on comfortably. That's why you need to be careful about retiring early. You want to make sure you get back every penny you put into the system.

14.

Give It Away

AN ENGLISH CLERGYMAN NAMED Thomas Fuller[72] is credited with the expression, "Charity begins at home, but should not end there." That's a lot better than the expression we all know which is just the first half. The more-common one almost appears as an argument against charity. Hey, you take care of your family first, the heck with everyone else.

The problem with that is a family always has needs or, at least, wants. Paying for aging parents or saving for your children's education can both sap your resources. Just handling the day-to-day sometimes seems too much.

Still, you need to give to charity.

If you are religious, you could give to your church or house of worship. If you aren't, pick some nonprofits that align with your beliefs. Care for the homeless or help fight the scourge of slavery around the world. There are plenty of problems you can choose from. Pick one. Or several.

And if you can't give money, and believe me brother, I've been there, then give of yourself. Donate your time, your ideas, you strong hands or big mouth and give others the help they need. This has to be a core value for everyone and our nation to stay united or for our people to stay who they are.

I promised myself when I started writing this book, that I wouldn't turn this chapter into what young folks call a humble brag on my own giving.

I have given to many different charities over the years, but I'm far from unique. It's the American way.

I give to my church because I and tens of millions in the U.S. like me think that's a good idea. According to Giving USA's[73] "2017: The Annual Report on Philanthropy for the Year 2016," Americans gave $390 billion in charity last year. That's more than the entire budget for all but 12 nations. More than the entire budgets of nations like Russia or South Korea.

You have my permission to laugh when you hear people on the news say Americans aren't charitable.

My Mother taught me that a person is only as good as how he or she treats others. The Good Samaritan from the Bible took care of a man he didn't know, but who lay beaten by the side of the road. He didn't ask for a tax break or demand to be acknowledged for his good deed. He simply did it because it needed to be done.

God has given us all things that we should share with those who are not as fortunate as we may be. He gives us the means to do things that need to be done. Yet, it's easy to get wrapped up in our own lives. You might want a new car or a nice piece of jewelry. You'll still be able to afford them, it just might take a little bit longer. Meanwhile, you'll feel better about yourself and you'll be helping others.

We were not a wealthy family growing up. That never stopped Dad giving money to a long line of people who needed a hand up. Dad was more than happy to help people in need, but he expected or even demanded that the person also be doing whatever he or she could do, as well. His reputation in Monahans was always one of charity and good will as a result. My Mom was much the same way. She was always giving things to those who needed them.

I think a main reason for their giving natures was the fact that they were both brought up during the Great Depression. Those were hard times and the people who lived through it did so by giving and getting help. Those of us who are older remember the TV show "The Walton's." It depicted a Depression era family coping with those struggles. Their neighbors helped them get by and they helped their neighbors do the same.

My parents instilled that nature in their children—even my little sister Kay. They truly believed that what you gave to others comes back to you at some point in the future. Maybe not in this life, but in the afterlife. I am convinced that they were right.

Acts 20:35 quoted Jesus saying: "It is more blessed to give than to receive." Jesus didn't say that it wasn't blessed to receive. Sometimes that's even harder, to just take a gift or even a compliment. Doing both well is important.

It has always been my belief that the things we "possess" aren't truly our own. Oh, I don't mean you can knock on my door and take my TV. This is Texas and I'd object—strongly. I mean they are gifts from God and we are supposed to tend and care for then while we are here as we do with our children.

When God gave man dominion over the earth, it wasn't just the beasts and fish, it was everything. We are called upon to be good stewards of ourselves, each other and the world around us.

By that, I mean we should share with those who may not be as fortunate as we are. My Mom and Dad were always willing to open the doors to our home to those who had a need to be filled.

I've tried to do the same. Not just at Thanksgiving or Christmas. People need help the other 363 days of the year, too.

Like many Christians, and many of other faiths as well, my church has always been my primary charity. Like most of you, I have been involved with many other nonprofit ventures over the years. Here are some of the major ones. I want you to see yourself when you read. Are these the kind of charities you want to support or do they make you think of others?

Susan and I have worked closely with MARC, the Midland Association for Retarded Citizens, following the birth of Erin, our daughter who has Down syndrome. We've tried to do more than just send a check. I served on the board of directors for that outstanding organization for several years.

As Erin grew older, we saw her need for specialized education and looked for groups that could help us. We became involved with the Bynum School, a private nonprofit here in Midland that provides education and direction to those who have developmental deficiencies.

The Bynum School[74] led us to assist with the Special Olympics, where both Susan and I worked for many years. Our time and some of our contributions were spent assisting with this program. They have repaid us many times over with their excellent work.

Most business people end up involved in a variety of community groups. They strengthen your ties to the neighbors you already serve and are a nice way of giving back to the community.

The North Midland YMCA has grown to be one of the centers of activity in the less-fortunate area of Midland. I've always loved the Y, even before the song came out. I was a board member for and worked with the youth program there, as we worked toward building a much-needed youth center and gymnasium.

Chambers of commerce are the lifeblood of any local business community and I have been a member of the Midland Chamber of Commerce for over thirty years, as well as a member of the Downtown Lions' Club. I've always been happy to lend a hand wherever either of these two fine organizations needed it. (I'm hoping no one is taking notes right now or my schedule will get even busier.)

I also serve as a board member of the Scranton Academy for Financial Education,[75] a nonprofit organization that provides financial education for young people and adults who need help learning how to handle their money and providing for the financial futures of their families. We conduct free seminars at the library and in the schools with the thought that more education in financial matters will make the lives of our citizens better and more financially sound. This fills a need that I think schools are no longer willing to handle.

I also try to address educational problems with my support of my alma mater, Abilene Christian, which I've already described. I am a member of the Champions Circle there, a group of men and women interested in supporting the athletic programs at the university. We have all made financial and time commitments to attract top-notch, Christian athletes and loved every minute of it.

It's not exactly Elvis, but I am also a board member for the Midland Odessa Symphony and Chorale, serving on the Sponsorship Committee raising funds for our outstanding chorale and orchestra.

And I told you about how important the Permian Basin Honor Flight Committee[76] is to me. I'm a member and I assist with the fundraising to send our World War II and Korean War veterans on free trips to Washington, D.C. to visit the memorials built in their honor. There aren't enough ways to say "Thank you" to those awesome men.

One of the most important charities for both Susan and me is the Cystic Fibrosis Foundation. Our youngest daughter Mandee has battled this genetic disease for many years. CF attacks the lung tissue and can eventually destroy it with bacterial infection.

Mandee was already seven when we discovered that she had the problem. It turned our lives upside down. It is hard to explain how difficult it is for parents, coping with the challenges posed by awful diseases that afflict their children. It is far more overwhelming for the children. Yet Mandee has handled it with grace.

I promised God soon after the diagnosis that I would give away all of the profits from any of my entertaining gigs to the Cystic Fibrosis Foundation. I have lived up to that promise without hesitation. The research people at the foundation have put that money to excellent use. They helped discover a drug that Mandee can take that helps her lung function to such an extent that Mandee has joined my business and we expect her to have a long life in service to our clientele.

God is Good!

It took a lifetime to do, get involved in all those organizations. If your list is smaller, just relax. It will probably put mine to shame in no time at all. If you commit to it.

I've had years to think of what people need to know about donating to charity. Here are some of the best ideas I've either discovered or taken from others. Here are eight tips so you do right by your charity and yourself.

1. **Give To Something You Care About:** This seems basic. Don't just donate to random charities because others are doing so. That doesn't give you any sense of involvement and it involves zero commitment, as well.

   Start small if you are just getting around to giving. Take stock of your interests and pick a charity. One is enough. See if it feels right. Would you be proud to tell others about it? If the answer is yes, it's a good start.

2. **Budget For It:** Budget for everything. You budget for charity the way you budget for your summer vacation. If you commit to spending the money, it's a lot easier to stick to it.

   Be sure it's on your budget spreadsheet, either as a percentage of what you take home or just a flat number. If all you can afford is $5, put that. One day, you'll be able to afford more. You are getting in the giving habit for now.

3. **Make Sure Your Charity Is Legit:** Famous investor Peter Lynch[77] has said "invest in what you know." Charity is a form of investing, so that advice applies the same way. My Dad might have said, "Don't buy a pig in a poke." Know what you are getting into.

   Talk to others you know who might know something about the charity. If you give to your church, maybe there's something specific you can fund that matters to you. No matter what it is, talk to people involved. Then do your due diligence online. Google it. Look it up on GuideStar[78] and Charity Navigator.[79] If it's not legitimate, you'll find out quickly.

4. **Pick A Smaller Charity:** If you want to have impact, give your money to an organization that needs it. Harvard University's endowment has more than $30 billion. Yes, that was a "B." Yale's endowment is paltry by comparison. It's just over $20 billion. They don't need your money. You could give them $100 million and they'd barely notice.

   Give to a smaller charity and, believe me, they'll notice. Give even $500 to most smaller groups and you'll hear from them. Make it $1,000 and I'd almost guarantee it. Because they see you as someone who can help them even more.

5. **Donate directly:** Don't donate through the United Way or other groups that share the money to the participating groups. That's not a knock on the United Way. It's just a way of making a connection.

   Donate directly to the group you plan to support. Get to know them and have them get to know you. Build a rapport. Find out about their needs. Maybe you know others you might be able to get involved.

6. **Give more than money:** Let me restate this point. We all have direct abilities to give. No matter how much money you have, try to give your time as well. Become more than just a checkbook to them. Volunteer.

   Think about the skills you have or maybe even want to learn. Offer your help and time. Go to events and see how they interact. You'll quickly get a sense of whether you've made the right choice or not.

7. **Donate Goods, Too:** Charities have lots of needs. The better you know them, the better you can help. Small charities need almost everything—office supplies, furniture, used computer equipment, a used car to make deliveries.

   And if they don't need those things, give them to Goodwill or other charities that will pick them up from your home. Try to commit to doing this at least twice a year, cleaning out what you don't want or maybe just don't need. Put it to good use.

8. **Yes, Take The Tax Deduction:** I give financial advice. I'm no accountant, but mine would yell at me if I didn't take the deduction. You aren't giving to get it, you'd still lose money in the long run. You are giving because it's the right thing to do. You are taking the tax deduction because it's your right under the tax laws.

   And no, don't lie about it. Don't be like someone famous I won't name and take a $2 write off for each piece of used undergarments. Be honest.

DEE'S DIRECTIVES:

Finding Security
In Social Security.

Now that you know you will be relying in part on Social Security for your retirement, there is still time to learn how to best manage it. Let me restate a few things, because they are important. Work as long as you reasonably can afford to work. That will help you earn the most from your salary level and by receiving the highest payment possible.

It takes just ten years of earning to qualify for Social Security. So there are benefits to taking a job later in life if you never worked before. It might make more sense, though, to file for spousal benefits if you are married to a big earner.

More experienced workers will want to stick around because the later years of your career can be peak earning years. And the payout you would get at age 70 is a lot higher than what you'd get at 62.

Remember, those payouts only change when you get a cost-of-living raise from Uncle Sam. If you take retirement at 62, it won't go up magically at 67 and 70 years of age.

Poor health is a good reason to claim early. But if you are healthy, it might be wise to wait. Imagine running out of your investments and having to live solely on Social Security for your remaining years. That's the kind of scenario many seniors I know fear most.

The Social Security Administration is incredibly busy. It's a good idea to learn to navigate its website. You'll find many handy tools there, including a life expectancy calculator. (I bet you can't wait to use that.) It includes an important qualifier that the estimates don't account for: "a wide number of factors such as current health, lifestyle, and family history that could increase or decrease life expectancy." In other words, if you are healthy and your family lives into their 90s, you'd better plan to do the same.

There are a ton of other nuances about Social Security and let me synopsize a few from their site.

I can't address them all here:

- For example, you can file for spousal benefits if you are divorced and haven't remarried. And there's nothing your ex-can do about it.
- Social Security isn't tax free. The federal government factors it into your taxable earnings. So do 13 states—from Colorado to West Virginia. It pays to figure out where your state lands.
- Earn enough other money and Government can tax your Social Security as income.
- Yes, you can change your mind after your first file for benefits—as long as you do it within 12 months of filing.
- You can file for survivors benefits before you hit 62. Don't wait.[80]

This is part of your holistic view of your retirement. Social Security is a guaranteed benefit and you can look up your estimated payment online. Between that and your other financial resources, you will know how much you should have to spend in retirement. If you live in a high-tax state—New York or California, for instance—you might consider relocating.

Wealth With
A Purpose

THE SERMON ON THE MOUNT gives some advice about how obsessed we become in our quest for money. Even though I advise people on how to manage what they earn and grow it, I never want my clients to get too focused on it.

There are two quotes that I think address that quite well. Matthew 6:19 says, "Do not store up for yourselves treasures on earth, where moths and vermin destroy, and where thieves break in and steal." It's a reminder that whatever we have here, our greatest reward is in heaven. I believe that with all my heart.

The other is even clearer. It's Matthew 6:24: "No one can serve two masters. Either you will hate the one and love the other, or you will be devoted to the one and despise the other. You cannot serve both God and money."

I don't want you to serve money. I want what you have spent a lifetime earning, scrimping and saving to serve you. The greatest mistake we all make is that we kill ourselves working and getting our paychecks 40, 50, 60 and more hours each week and then spend no time at all managing what we have gathered.

Think about that. You spend 2,000 hours a year or more, and sometimes a lot more, earning your money. How much do you spend making sure you manage it correctly? Sure you pay your bills. And maybe you spend a little time on stocks, but how much? One hour a week? Two?

And if you do spend the time, other things suffer. This section is about how to do all that differently than you were taught.

Simply put: There is a better way.

A better way to invest. A better way so you can embrace your retirement and do the things you've always wanted to do. A better way so you leave a legacy for your loved ones.

This is what I preach now.

15.

Go Tell It
On The Mountain

IT'S FUNNY HOW RIGHT some people can be. When my uncle the
preacher told an entire church that I was going to preach for my
career, I thought he was crazy. My life took some twists and turns,
but I ended up doing precisely that.

I'm not just a financial advisor. I'm a financial evangelist. My role
in life is to help you live your life to the fullest—during your career
and, especially, in your retirement. When I do my work, the time
that I put in has to be filled with love of what I do and the love of the
people that walk through that door. I want them to feel that.

This work is not a job. It's a calling. It's a ministry. I'm still min-
istering to the needs of my clients in a very similar way to the way I
handled my parishioners. Because the people who come in my office
are just the same kind of people who came into my office when I was
a minister. They are people who need help, sometimes a lot more than
just financial.

Financial problems often are spurred by other events—medical
emergencies, lost jobs, children going to college or your retirement.
Many of them are good news. Having your only child accepted into

Harvard is sure to be a moment of great pride for any parent. It might take a minute, but then you realize you have to pay for it.

Some of those times are quite challenging. I don't know how many hours a week I spend just sitting and talking with my clients. One client lost her husband and I've been helping her through what that means financially—insurance, estate and lots of paperwork. And it's hard. I can't imagine how hard. After we finished discussing her situation, she just wanted to keep talking.

She needed a shoulder to lean on or cry on. And I wanted to be there for her. I didn't make a dime off that. But she knows I'm helping her reach her financial goals and walking her through her emotional goals too.

That's plenty of payment for me.

Another of my clients sent me a note a while back saying that she had lots of spots on her lungs. And she just had surgery and now she has to go to MD Anderson to get a second opinion. I sent her a little note telling her I was praying for her. I told her I would be there for her, to help her with her finances and just to be there as a friend.

To me, this business is more than just dollars and cents. It has to be. It's got to be time and love, as well.

My practice isn't like what many advisors have. I don't try to handle the number of appointments many of them do. It's not how I operate. And it's not how I want to operate.

I try to find a client that I can work with and that appreciates my approach. If I can't tell a client, "You go home and pray about this," then I am probably the wrong advisor to work with that person. You can probably do that more in Texas than most anywhere.

Texas is proudly part of the Bible Belt and I'm happy about that.

People come in so beaten down by the markets, even sometimes in good years. But always in bad years. "We were ready to retire and we lost half our money in the stock market," I've been told. It's like their whole world has caved in on them.

Everything they've been taught about investing has blown up in their face and there's no one there to help them.

That's where I come in. I always ask if their broker contacted them. The typical answer is a firm, "No." In their defense, that's the way they're taught. That's on their companies and less on the advisors, who are usually really good people.

There just are better ways to do this.

The problem is that even the experts need to learn how to do better. They simply aren't taught that there are better options.

When I first got my Series 6 securities license in 1974, when I moved to California, I was taught to say things a certain way. They're still teaching the same way. I tell my clients things need to be different. I pull out a dotcom expression and tell them: "You have to change your paradigm." I go on to explain that they are reaching a stage in their lives where they need to change how they invest.

If you reach sixty years of age and you continue in the growth market, you are setting yourself up for a dangerous potential downside. If you continue the growth market and there's maybe a five percent chance that you could make money, but there's a twenty-five percent chance that you could lose money, are you willing to risk it? Are you willing to risk five percent on the upside for twenty-five percent on the down? You are setting yourself up to fail.

What we were taught as advisors is: "Don't worry, the market always comes back." OK, but what if I don't live long enough for it to come back? What happens to me and my family and my retirement plans if I lose fifty percent of my investments? That means I've got to make a hundred percent back just to break even.

It took six years to get from the peak of October 10th 2007—14,165.02 on the Dow—to March 6th 2013, when it hit a new high of 14,253.77, according to Yahoo Finance[81]. If you had your money in the market the whole time, you broke even with the Dow and lost money because of inflation. Sure, you might feel like you had good years. Once the market started rebounding, it had lots of up days.

We tend to forget the down days. And there were a lot of them.

The Dow plummeted from its peak all the way down to 6,443.27, according to The Houston Chronicle[82]. A drop of fifty-four percent in just seventeen months. People lost jobs. Families lost homes. And while the markets have recovered, many of those impacted have not. What if you died in the middle of that, how would your family survive? What if your job loss forced you to liquidate your investments?

Economies recover. Some people profited. Others lost everything.

It didn't have to be that way. What if they had chosen a different path? What if they met me and decided to put their investments into fixed-income products? Then they don't have to endure the market turmoil. They're back at where they were and then they double their investment.

They're in great shape—without the same risk of the market.

Don't get me wrong. I'm not against the stock market. I'm licensed to do it and it makes sense for a great number of people. It doesn't make sense for everyone. We use the market with income products and I'm happy to do it. The stuff that we do is relatively safe by comparison. We're talking about high-yield bonds that make sense in a portfolio.

I didn't say bond funds. I hate bond funds. People come into to see me and tell me how they've put all their money in bond funds, because it's safer. I ask: Oh really? Was your rate of interest guaranteed? Investors don't realize that bond funds don't have a guaranteed rate of interest or a guaranteed maturity date.

Put it in bonds, in real bonds, and you will have a guaranteed rate of interest and a guaranteed maturity date. Individual bonds. I had a client ask about this and he wanted to see the types of returns. I showed him and his response was, "Oh my word!"

This isn't what any of us has been taught about the stock market. It's a total change in attitude. It's getting away from the greed and fear. That's really what were here for and that's why I have to push it to people just like a ministry.

Our client base is very diverse. We have clients who own oil companies or who work for them. We have clients who work for food stores and service stations and we have small businessmen who really keep West Texas moving. They come from all walks of life.

But the bottom line is eighty percent of the economy here is built on petroleum. If oil dries up, so does money for most everything else. And whether the price is up or down, the core group of people who keep that oil flowing will have jobs. And they will need to find a place to put their money for retirement.

That keeps me busy in good times or bad.

Probably seventy-five percent of my clients either work for oil companies or have somebody in their families that do work for the industry somewhere in the oil patch. So, I need to speak their language. When oil hits $50, we have a lot of paper millionaires and the U.S. Energy Information Administration tracks all this. It can go a lot higher. In 2008, it went as high as $127 a barrel. Along with the peaks, you get the valleys. When it drops to $30, we have a lot of folks who want to jump out of buildings. It hit $8 a barrel in 1998-99, just before the dotcom crash. Those were bad times in West Texas.[83]

There were a lot of vacant buildings in Midland when that collapse happened. Many of the companies that had their headquarters here, moved to Houston. It just didn't make sense to stay here, it wasn't feasible. They even shut down a lot of the wells. They were losing too much money pumping oil for $8 a barrel. It cost more to produce the oil than they were making. It wasn't until they discovered horizontal drilling that things began to rebound here.

All that means the people I work with often have their own boom-and-bust cycles.

One of my clients called me on the phone a while back talking about his portfolio and we ended up discussing the oil price. I asked him about his financial situation and how much money he had in his checking and savings accounts. He said he had about $10 million.

I was shocked and asked him why. He said, "I'm drilling three wells. Ask me again in three months." In three months, that $10 million was long gone. But the wells got drilled. It costs a lot of money to drill. A lot of those wells around Midland are pretty deep and that is expensive. When things are going right, oil rigs are in use. When the price is low, those rigs are stacked in the yard, waiting. Picture a big work yard filled with trucks and rigs, stored for when times get better.

Even with that, we live in a little bubble in Midland. There's a lot of oil wealth here and you have to drive a ways before you get to the nearest city of any size. That drives the wealth of our area into Midland-Odessa and sometimes right to my doorstep.

Despite the differences, West Texas is just like every place in America. Whether Texans or New Yorkers, Marylanders or Georgians, we're all taught the same set of rules. Only, when it comes to the stock market, we've all been taught incorrectly.

People are learning there's a better way and I sure hope I'm part of that.

I had done radio and TV commercials off and on for years, but that all changed when I met Craig and Doris Anderson. Craig owns KWEL radio in the heart of Midland. We started working together and he complimented me on my voice.

The next thing I knew, I was doing a weekly appearance on the radio show, talking about whatever was on my mind, but always turning things back to finances. Always trying to teach people that they don't have to ride the stock market roller coaster with their entire life savings. Evangelizing.

I didn't see a lot of activity for the first three or four months. I think listeners were trying to get my measure. Then, all of a sudden, I started getting calls. I do a mix of commercials that go along with my show. I think the combination really works teaching people and getting them inspired to call me. I'd bet half my business comes from the radio, now.

That's a great way to start because when we finally meet, they already feel like they know me. They also know what I believe, what I think about investing. That's what brought them to me. Because people have been burned and they are tired of it. Either they've lost money in the downturns or missed out on the upside.

A lot of people have also the FOMO thing, the Fear of Missing Out. The guy down the street just bought this stock and he's making a ton and I want to do the same thing. It ends up being the herd instinct.

It's keeping up with the Jones. My neighbor has a new car, so I have to have a new car. My best friend has a new house, so I start house hunting, even though I love where I live. They are chasing dreams that often turn into nightmares. They know it, they just don't know how to stop.

They are looking for a better way. And that's why we're here. To provide them with a different way to look at investing their money.

People want a better way invest because they are tired of the fear, the threats to their savings. I'm sure of it.

I think it's because people have been through the boom-and-bust cycle a few times. I've been through three of them. People learn, even if it takes getting hit over the head with a copy of *The Wall Street Journal* a few thousand times. We learn. The folks I work with are more discerning now. When they make the money now, they aren't just throwing it away on big houses at the country club.

One of my friends owned a small oil company. He got wealthy in the 1980s and 1990s and when the bust came, it hit hard. He had built a big home out on one of the country clubs and didn't have enough money to pay the taxes on his home the next year. That's how bad it got. He had to sell his Rolex to pay the taxes.

I know. Young people would laugh and call that "first world problems" and they're right. Things aren't that bad if you can keep your house in lean times, even if you do lose a fancy timepiece. Most people don't enjoy that and the next time they have money, they are more careful with it.

Thankfully, the more people wise up, the more they turn to financial professionals like me. People come to us and say, "I just made $500,000 and I don't want to lose it all again. What do I do with the money?"

They're in the right place. We'll do our best to ensure that it's invested safely. There are no guarantees in life. But caution is one of our watch words.

How we handle that from there on depends on how safe the client wants to be. Other companies talk about "risk tolerance." I don't even use those words. I'm a bit more subtle. I use "threshold of pain." Believe me, when you drop that phrase, people pay attention. When it starts to hurt, it's time to do something about it.

So when I used to talk about "risk tolerance," that didn't mean squat to people. But when I ask, "What's your threshold of pain when it comes to money," they know what I mean. At what point does it start to hurt. Is that any loss? Is it ten percent? Twenty? At what point does it get so bad that you want something done?

I think another reaction to the boom-and-bust cycle in oil is that the threshold of pain has gotten higher and higher. People can handle it, but they also know what to do about it.

They turn to experts. And I hope that means they turn to me.

Even experts need expert help. When I first encountered Dave Scranton and the Advisors' Academy, I thought I was a prophet crying alone in the wilderness. I'd been pushing people to get out of the traditional market since 2001. I figured I was the only one. At the time, everybody was shouting: "Greed, greed, greed, greed!" And the market was falling from the dotcom crash. I thought they were crazy.

Getting to that realization was hard for me. I was working for another company and I literally cried myself to sleep at nights because my clients were losing money and I didn't have any solutions for them.

Finally, I quit. I couldn't keep selling them the same products and the same stock market that I knew didn't work for them. I knew there had to be a better solution. It was all making me sick.

That's no exaggeration. I had stopped refereeing and I didn't even have time to work out. The weight gain was immense, at least 40 pounds. I was on high blood pressure medication. My whole system was a wreck. I was close to sixty and felt ten years older.

I went to see my doctor, who was also a client of mine. He performed my annual physical and started asking tough questions. "How old was your Dad when he had his first stroke?" I knew what he was getting at instantly and it cut through me like a knife.

I mumbled, "62," staring down at the floor. He shook his head: "You'll never make it." He pointed out the paper he had been filling out with my blood pressure and other information. "You're a time bomb. You have to lose forty to fifty pounds just for starters."

That was only the symptom, he said. So then he continued. "I'll make another suggestion you might think is crazy. You're not happy with your job and where you're at in life. You need to find something that you can be happy doing or else."

The doc and I knew each other pretty well. Our daughters were cheerleaders together and we were each other's client, as well. So I listened hard to what he told me. I thought about it the whole way home. When I got there, I told Susan I need to lose forty pounds and I need to change occupations.

There was a look of relief that came over Susan. Instead of worrying about how we were going to pay the bills or how a man sixty years old goes job hunting, she was thrilled. I didn't realize how difficult I was to live with at that point in my life. I was bringing home my clients' woes and I was in such a funk, I was dumping them on Susan.

Things had to change. For me, for my family, and, most importantly, for my clients.

Susan and I prayed about it for the next month or so. I gave it serious consideration because, in my heart, I knew the doctor was right. I had to find something else. I could do a lot of jobs, except being a car dealer. Susan didn't want any part of that life. But I knew I could find something. The question was what? I even considered going to work for an oil company in Midland. But that just wasn't what I wanted to do.

That was just another job. That's a livelihood, that's not a life. My whole career, I had tried to do jobs that inspired me. I wanted something that was doing good and, at the same time, would compensate me for what I was doing.

I was the general agent at the time, in charge of an office handling Midland-Odessa and Lubbock. Seventeen agents reported to me and I probably made more than all of them put together. It was a tough thing to walk away from.

I talked to my accountant about it and he had the oddest response. He said: "Let me show you something." He pointed to my tax forms and explained. "If you didn't have all his overhead, you'd be making $50,000 more a year."

I decided to quit as a manager. I stayed a representative for two more years, selling mutual funds and variable life insurance—all things we were doing back in those days. I couldn't keep doing that.

When I got ready to quit, I took my 401(k) money in the bank and paid the taxes on it. Then I took the rest and plowed it into IRAs. Then I started looking for a new way to make a living.

That lasted for seven months. I looked everywhere. I went to companies from Atlanta to Sacramento. Everywhere I went, I would interview with the group and have them tell me why I needed to work for them, what they could do for my clients.

I kept finding the nuggets of an idea that made sense to me. I found companies were using fixed-income products and learned how they worked. I thought about it and couldn't find anything wrong with participating in the growth but not participating in the downside.

That's like flipping a coin and heads you win and tails you break even. I figured that's better than tails you lose. So I came back and lined up with four or five companies and started the Carter Financial Group in 2001.

I did that by myself for 10 years until I discovered Advisors' Academy. Or I should say, until they discovered me. Dave sent me a copy of his book. I was being recruited at least once a week by different companies. Everybody said the same spiel: We've got a better mousetrap.

None of them did. Until I met Dave Scranton.

He's got a mind that can grasp a problem and go to a solution faster than anyone I've ever met. And he's twenty-five years younger than me. But when we got together the first time, it was like we'd known each other for years. We spent the day together talking about the business and how I could fit in with the Advisors' Academy. We ended up spending the end of the day looking at a boat because another guy was considering buying it.

When I got home, I read Dave's book and gave it to Susan. She had the most-amazing reaction. Susan said, "You need to work with that man." She's still giving me the advice about the people with whom she wants me to work after all these years!

She didn't just mean that for me. She meant it for my clients. They're like family to us. She knew he could help me help them.

Now, when I meet with a new client, I don't just focus on how much they have and how much they need to retire. Sure, I use those points. Everybody does. My biggest thing is, what do you want to do when you get to retirement? And can I help you achieve that goal as safely as possible?

What I do is simple. I take my client's concerns about stocks and investing and we try to solve them together. You've got to love what you do to make a life out of it. You make a living, but it's work.

This isn't making a living. This is making a life for me and all my clients.

Let me tell you how.

DEE'S DIRECTIVES:

Just What You Wanted, A New Acronym—Meet The RMD.

There are many complex aspects to retirement financial planning. One of the most important and difficult involves Required Minimum Distributions—the RMD from the headline. It's also unfortunately the one we are least prepared to handle. We've grown up around Social Security and have family members receiving benefits. That gives us a foundation of knowledge.

RMDs are far different and the odds are you are just learning about them. The term RMD refers to the employer-sponsored retirement accounts that the government has encouraged you to fund. These include your 401(k)/403(b) and similar accounts that fall under the heading of IRAs.

The government mandates that you have to start taking these at the age of 70½. Here's the IRS's wording about when you turn 70 ½. "You reach age 70½ on the date that is 6 calendar months after your 70th birthday." If you don't take the money out when you are supposed to, the IRS can penalize you 50 percent. (There's also a form to get out of this penalty.) Roth IRAs are different and don't require withdrawals until after the death of the owner.

The complexity of timing and taxes makes RMDs a huge headache for your average taxpayer. To do it properly, you have to juggle how much you plan to take out from each, as well as other instruments like annuities. It's too complex to detail all of it here. Think of this section as a starter kit.

You need a different government life expectancy table called the Uniform Lifetime Distribution table to figure out how much you need to deduct from your RMD each year. You have to do a separate calculation for each account, but can remove the money from any of them. This is an annual calculation. If all this looks exciting to you, expect to do it each year. Or make sure your advisor does it.

Your retirement contributions were tax deductible when you made them. They don't stay that way forever. But your tax rate depends on which tax brackets you fall into. Yes, I said brackets. Not bracket. And the payouts from your RMDs can impact how much of your Social Security gets taxed, too. If you don't want to pay taxes on the money and would rather donate it, there's a way of directly transferring it to the IRS-approved charity you want.

One option that cuts down on complexity is using your IRA to purchase an annuity. You get either a set or variable income stream from the annuity, but delete the RMD insanity that you don't want to handle. There are reasons for each type of annuity, depending on your financial situation.

I'll be honest. Even trying to synopsize RMDs makes me tired and I deal with them every day. They are complicated financial instruments and need to work in conjunction with all of your other income—Social Security, investments, salary, etc.—to keep you from getting hammered on taxes.

If you hadn't been listening about the need for a financial advisor up till now, listen.

16.

If You've Got
The Money

MY INVESTING PHILOSOPHY IS simple and straightforward. I read a book about Warren Buffet's business strategy. He said it better than I could. "Rule No. 1 is never lose money. Rule No. 2 is never forget Rule No. 1." Anything other than that is extra.

Our idea of finance has changed a lot in my lifetime. People used to set aside money in savings accounts or even Christmas accounts. Now, you need to invest just to stay ahead of inflation. Savings accounts don't do that. The top savings rates, as I write this, are around 1.5% thanks to the trackers at NerdWallet.[84] Inflation always stays ahead of those rates. So, you need other options.

Many customers try mutual funds. The money magazines push those as simple alternatives to clients who don't know how to invest. But even they require management and understanding of fees and monitoring the market. That's more than many people want to deal with.

And either way, you are still in the stock market. Forget the market recovery. Go back and look at some of those mutual fund results from 2008-2009. Imagine that hit again and, instead of a fairly quick recovery, it takes ten to fifteen years. Where will you be in that time?

If you are sixty now, just contemplating retirement, that would make you seventy or seventy-five. Meanwhile, you're trying to live all that time with your savings chopped in half or worse.

To avoid all that, many people turn to professionals. My clients, and the clients for almost any financial advisor, are above-average savers. According to the Economic Policy Institute, nearly half of all Americans have no retirement savings. None.

Let that rattle around in your brain for a second. Sure, some of them are younger and figure they'll save when they hit peak earnings. But even among those who do save, the median they have to count on is $60,000. If you have more than that, you go to the head of the class. As long as you have saved something, you have the potential to do better for yourself in retirement. You also deserve to pat yourself on the back.

If you want an advisor, it helps finding one you can trust, who understands both the markets and what clients want.

Explaining all that and giving you a basic understanding of what's entailed takes a lot. So buckle up, this will be the book's longest and most-important chapter.

Investment advice requires stringent requirements, training, examinations, licenses and more. Financial advisors have a whole pile of rules we have to obey, what we can, what we can't say and do and when. (There are even people poring over every page of this book to make sure I don't break any rules.)

It only makes sense that advisors be of the finest caliber. Any black mark at all can hinder your career for life. Let me tell you what I mean, so you understand what I went through to get here.

I mentioned earlier about playing with Roy Orbison on July 4th in beautiful Kermit, Texas. I didn't tell you how I spent that same night in jail. And the regulators are so thorough that more than 50 years later, they still tried to run the story to ground.

The band and I ran into a couple airmen we knew from the nearby radar base. They asked if they could bum a ride with us back to Monahans. We were more than happy to have more company, even if it did make a bit of a tight squeeze in the car—the band, the instruments and now two airmen. I figured we'd manage. The one airman and I had double-dated a few times. I figured there'd be no trouble if they joined us.

Only the next people to join us were the police. They had other ideas. It turned out that the airman I knew had stolen a fender skirt off of a car. Not just any car. It was the car owned by the owner of the hotel where we were eating. He also happened to be the mayor.

I swear, I expect to see this one written up in one of those Murphy's Law books.

Of course, the airman put the stupid fender skirt in my car to take it back to base. I never did know why he took it. I guess he needed a new one and was too cheap and stupid to buy it. The police showed up and they could see the part sitting in my back seat and they arrested us all—the two airmen and me and the other four members of the band. It was probably the biggest crime wave to hit Kermit in years.

I was livid. Not at the police. I couldn't really blame them. But I told them they better put us in separate cells because I wanted to kill him.

We all got a free night's room and board in the Kermit jail. At least they fed us—hot beef sandwiches for dinner. Breakfast was just steaming, black coffee. Kermit wasn't expecting us to stay.

Morning came and the air patrol picked up our friendly neighborhood crook. That was only the beginning of his problems. He was Airman Second Class and he got busted back to Airman and was confined to base for six months.

In some ways, he got off easy.

I had to call my Dad and that was only the beginning of my problems. He drove over to Kermit up Highway 18, probably spitting fire the whole way. First he got mad at me. Then when I explained, he got mad at the airman.

Dad was only getting warmed up.

He was determined to get it all sorted out. So we went and talked with the mayor. Turned out the mayor knew the band and I weren't guilty. But he told Dad he thought I could use a night in jail as a learning experience.

Dad was furious. He reached across the desk and grabbed the mayor by the collar and lifted him out of his chair. I rarely saw Dad angry and almost never like this. He stared the man down and said, almost daring the other guy to do something, "This is my son. I make the decisions for him. Not you." And then he dropped him back in the chair.

This was the mayor. I thought we were both going to spend the night in jail. But he was smart enough not to mess with my Dad. This was a man who fought Nazis. He wasn't afraid of a small town politician.

I wasn't guilty of anything at all, but that crazy incident would follow me around for more than 50 years—until 2017. The charges were dropped. Only Kermit authorities didn't expunge the record. That got complicated when I went to get my Series 7 license. If you don't get it expunged, it stays on there forever.

When you go to get a securities license, you have to get approved by the Financial Industry Regulatory Authority or FINRA. The question they ask is: Have you ever been convicted of a felony? They automatically deny you for a felony if it happened within 10 years. And they will also deny you for some misdemeanors.

Of course, I answered no. The FINRA folks are good at what they do. They came back to me and said, you didn't tell us about this arrest. I responded: "Well, you didn't ask me." Besides, it happened in high school and I wasn't convicted of anything.

I explained and they were great. They took care of everything we could take care of and he told me to fax him the letter showing how I wasn't convicted as soon as I got back.

That's how thorough FINRA is to give a securities license though I no longer have my Series 7 at this point.

That's only one part of what it takes to understand my professional life and really the professional life of anyone who you might want to manage your money. My company, the Carter Financial Group, has been in Midland since April 1, 1976. I just beat the bicentennial. As I write this, I'm coming up on my forty-second anniversary here. If you pay attention to wedding anniversary gifts, that means I'm supposed to buy myself some real estate. I can assure you, it won't be in a retirement community. I don't think I'll ever be ready for that.

My business was affiliated with two large national life insurance firms for twenty-five years. But I finally had to cut ties. In 2000, I went independent because that offered me and, more importantly, my clients a wider range of investments and insurance options. That last part is key. As a financial advisor, it's never about you. It's always the clients and what they want or need.

From that point on, we became a "stand alone" entity, affiliated with top companies to give my clients the investments I think they need. Those have included both fixed-income and bond-like investment opportunities.

We kept growing our business and, in 2017, I even became an IAR (Investment Advisory Representative) with Sound Income Strategies, an SEC-Registered Investment Advisory Firm (RIA) that stressed investing for income.

That was only the latest professional feather in my cap. I became a Registered Representative in 1974 and later earned the Chartered Life Underwriter, Chartered Financial Consultant and Registered Financial Consultants designations.

I was also one of the first recipients of the Certified Senior Advisor's designation. My daughter, Mandee, also works in my office as an associate and is training to take over one day.

I joined the Advisors' Academy in 2011. It's a very exclusive group of financial advisors and I like that. Dave Scranton's an author of two books on the subject of retirement planning, and one of those faces you see on CNBC and Fox Business a whole bunch. He's also the Founder of Sound Income Strategies.

I'm proud of those accomplishments. But I'm clearly not the only game in town. I've met some amazing people who are financial advisors. They have a long list of letters and words surrounding their names, too. I won't cut on one of them. Not one. The only problem is, we disagree about how to handle money. I am as conservative with my clients' money as I am with my own and many of them want to be more aggressive. The problem is, as I see, it's not their money.

It's yours.

And that gets to the heart of everything I want to say about investing in this book. The financial services industry—advisors, tip sheets, news outlets, mutual funds, the whole deal—is focused on huge returns. To get huge returns, you have to take huge risk.

Let me put it another way. Almost the entire industry wants you to take everything you've saved for your entire life and put it in a craps game called the stock market. Don't do it and they tell you that your foolish. What they don't tell you is that they are rolling the dice, but it's your money they are gambling with.

Turn on CNBC and you'll see "experts" obsessed with how tech stocks are doing today. Gosh, Apple is tearing things up. Or Google. Or there's a merger that sent these four stocks skyrocketing. Or maybe some stock is down. Oh no! Should you sell? If you've never been in a casino, it looks just like this.

There's tons of noise and activity, people yelling, making money and losing it. There are flashing lights and bright colors and everyone smiles even when you just lost everything. Because the house always wins.

If you look at the graphics and the energy, it's reminiscent of one of those video slot machines. And the only way to win is to score really big. You have to beat everyone else.

The universe of financial advice is built entirely on this dynamic. It doesn't sell you returns or security or advice. The industry sells greed or fear. The greed part is easy. It's everywhere like a heavy cologne someone sprayed on too much. If you even get near it, it gets on your clothes, gets in your nostrils. You can smell the greed, taste it even. The whole goal is to make you feel left out unless you buy, buy, buy!

The fear industry is almost as bad. It's much smaller and lacks national TV outlets to promote it. Its goal is to tell you an apocalypse is coming every single day. You have to buy gold or silver in that world. Don't get me wrong, I'm a big believer in being careful. I just don't let fear rule my life.

And you shouldn't let it rule yours either.

I always try to explain those things in terms people can understand when I meet with clients. Imagine you go to a car dealership to buy an SUV and the salesman brings you out a convertible. It's fantastic, bright red and could probably outrun the police that try to give you tickets. The engine sounds like it has more horsepower than 1,000 Kentucky Derbies. You shake your head no and tell him that's not what you want as it revs up to the curb.

He goes away and comes back with another convertible, only this one's white, so maybe it won't draw as much police attention. It still has a six-figure or even seven-figure engine, roaring like it is fed jet fuel. Only it's not what you want. You're confused and step outside and realize you are in a Ferrari dealership. You aren't in the right place!

Ferraris are fantastic cars, for the right place and circumstances. But they aren't an SUV. You want a vehicle that can get your family where it's got to go. Maybe seats five or more, has room for groceries, things you have to move, athletic equipment, you name it. The Ferrari is a two-seater. It's made for speed only. It doesn't fit your needs.

Investing is just like that. You can go to a stockbroker and they'll sell you that Ferrari that you don't want. Or you can come to Carter Financial and we'll sell you an SUV that seats five and doesn't have to be kept in a garage.

I use that illustration all the time. And it works most of the time. People understand it.

Sometimes they need a stronger lesson. Then, I tell the story about the B-24 my pilot friend flew. I met him on the Honor Flight heading to D.C. one year. He had gone out on a mission and bombed the daylights out of a place in Romania. His plane got so shot up that on the way back, he could barely keep it in the air. Every inch back to base, the wind ripped through the holes trying to tear the plane apart.

Finally, he got back to base. A miracle. He fought it every second of the way down till he was able to land, the plane pulling this way and that until it was at a dead stop. Once on the ground, he got out and his plane looked like Swiss cheese, only German made. They did the only thing they could think of. They started counting. When they were done, they counted 151 holes in the plane. One of the holes was the size of a basketball—right through the plane's rudder. I asked one eager client, would you get in a plane like that and fly it?

He nearly jumped out of his chair. "Absolutely not." I smiled: "That's the stock market we're talking about."

He got it. They always do. That one always works. You just have to paint the picture.

Let's talk about the stock market. If you are like most Americans, you've got some money tied up there in one form or another. A full fifty-four percent have some money there, reported Bloomberg.[85] And no wonder, there's tons of money to be made in stocks.

Unfortunately, a lot of small investors aren't the ones making it. Part of that reason is that the markets have so many bad actors. I'm not just talking Bernie Madoff. Sure, his little Ponzi scheme was worth $64 billion. And, sure, he used to be chairman of NASDAQ. But everything in the markets is on the up and up, we're told.

Think Enron, Fannie Mae, Lehman Brothers and a host of other major financial scandals. Banks alone have paid $321 billion in fines since the 2007-2008 collapse. More than $200 billion of that is in North American banks, according to the Boston Consulting Group. Bank of America has been fined three times and get this, $8.5 billion, $11.8 billion and $16.6 billion.[86]

It's fair to say the financial industry bigwigs have issues. And that mixture of greed, stupidity and pressure trickles down on to Wall Street. No wonder brokers get stressed. No wonder they push themselves hard and take risks. There are billions to be made for them and billions to be lost for their clients.

Even, up years in the market are tough on individual investors. And 2017 was absolutely insane—for investing and for politics, in part because they intersect. The markets were convinced for a long time that Congress was going to pass President Trump's tax bill in some form. The pundits kept saying they were wrong. At the end of 2017, instead of the markets repeating the 2007-2009 collapse, they boomed under the new President Donald Trump.

It's not smart to bet against Las Vegas and sometimes the stock market is just as savvy. A form of the Trump tax bill passed, meaning great things for businesses and taxpayers alike. The top business tax rate plummeted to 21 percent and four out of five taxpayers are also slated for a tax cut.

Having said that, I still feel that the clientele that I serve (mostly retirees and near-retirees) are better served by reducing their market risk. They should think "income" rather than "growth." Especially after such a major run up in the markets. Don't get too greedy.

We have opportunities through the Advisors' Academy and through Sound Income Strategies to solve most people's traditional investing problems and help to protect them as best we possibly can. That only operates within the framework of how well they want to be protected. If they want a more-aggressive approach, so be it. Not every client has the same attitude about their pain threshold.

Even when they want a more-aggressive approach, we're still giving you guidance about what we think is best, based on the last forty-five years of experience and looking at the market over its entire existence, not just since January. I can use my own experience and look back twenty to thirty years at someone who might have tried the exact same strategy.

And now, especially, I would counsel against that strategy.

I was on a panel several years ago following a presentation by Dr. Robert Shiller, the man who wrote "Irrational Exuberance." He was on to talk about the Case-Shiller Index. Dr. Shiller is one of those people who has a Bio that can take longer than five minutes to read and only scratch the surface. He's a Nobel Laureate, an economics professor at Yale University and a research associate for the National Bureau of Economic Research. Even famous people's bios rarely read like his.

He went out there and just killed it. And no wonder. He warned about the dotcom boom. His book was published in March of 2000. That same month the dotcom crash began. The NASDAQ, which is where a lot of the tech stocks are listed, peaked at just over 5,000 and dropped more than seventy percent by September of 2002.[87]

It left a big impact on me. I read his book several years ago and I just reread it because I think it's about to come into play. If the market's actions are based on the Case-Shiller Index, we need to worry. As I write this, the Case-Shiller U.S. National Home Price Index is notably higher than it was just before the 2007-2009 collapse. In fact, the only times that the Index has been higher than it is today is when the dotcom crash occurred in 2000 and, get this, October 13, 1929, when the Wall Street Crash washed out the savings of most Americans![88]

I can remember vividly, what happened to the advisors who abandoned their convictions with regard to income planning back in 2006 and 2007. The market did what the market does and dropped by fifty to sixty percent. That caused some devastating losses for clients who had not been encouraged to reduce their market risk prior to the collapse.

It's like everyone wants to squeeze every last penny out of a stock rise, rather than playing it conservatively and being satisfied with their good fortune.

That 2007-2009 disaster was the second major downturn in this century. If history is a teacher (and I firmly believe that it is), there have historically been three to five or six downturns before the market starts into what we recognize as a bull secular market.

You only have to look at the market's ups and downs since 1900 to realize that. Even though 2017 was an excellent year for stocks, we've really been in a bear secular market cycle since 2000. So far, we have only seen two downturns.

To quote my friend Dave Scranton, author of "Return On Principle, "This market was largely created by the Federal Reserve,[89] and is still hovering without fundamental support like a woman in a magician's trick." This year's tax cut added to that bit of legerdemain.[90]

Long-term rates are still not being driven up even though the Fed is still talking about increasing short-term interest rates. Plus, the

GDP (Gross Domestic Product) and the real un-employment figures have not entirely recovered to that pre-crash level, leaving the yield curve flat. (Real unemployment is pretty close at this writing, but not quite there.) Until those things get back to where they need to be, the investor needs to be extremely cautious. That is what is creating the yield curve that we have been discussing with our clientele for the past three years.

The year closed out with a bang, not a whimper. The Dow spiked 5,000 points for the first time in history. There is more money in the economy because unemployment is down and wages have increased slightly, but money for goods and services is still not being spent. And that's more than a bit worrisome.

The Baby Boomers are not spending and they are the ones with big money. Instead, they are saving and that does nothing to stimulate the GDP. It does keep money in the stock and the bond markets. When the yield curve flattens, watch out for the next market crash.

I know you're asking the simple question: "What's the solution?" My answer and the answer of the people I work with at the Advisors' Academy is not to play that game the same way everyone else is doing.

No, we're not recommending you put your money in the mattress or start digging holes in your yard, unless you are planning on planting come spring. There are ways that get you out of the day-to-day chaos of investing, that pay reliable returns and don't have you getting an ulcer or heartburn about your money.

I'll explain a little bit more about that. Let's start, though, by discussing retirement, which is a big chunk of the job of most financial advisors.

There are three major components of any retirement investing strategy—the money you already have invested or in savings, your pensions/retirement plans such as IRAs, 401(k)s, 403(b)s and Social Security. Pensions have gotten rare for new retirees, unless they work for government.

Most individuals tend to focus only on the first two. Savings accounts are a joke and I hope I've warned you enough about the stock market to be cautious. Too often retirement accounts, IRA, etc., are just other ways to jam as much money as possible into the hands of the folks on Wall Street. But they are also extremely complicated and have detailed rules about when you can or even when you have to take out money. To give you a hint how complex this is, the IRS rules page on their website has more than 2,400 words about how to do it.

That alone is an important reason to engage a financial professional. If you make the correct retirement moves, it can save you thousands of dollars. Make the wrong moves and you either miss out on benefits or incur more taxes. Who wants their retirement going to pay Uncle Sam?

Then there's the third category, Social Security. You paid into Social Security your whole working life. It's designed to be part of your retirement plan.

Notice I said "part" of your retirement. Not the whole thing. Too many Americans live in the here and now and haven't saved. They expect Social Security to take care of them completely when they retire and it's not designed that way.

They have a rude awakening coming their way.

Social Security is actually a lot more than just retirement. It includes disability and survivor payments. To figure out where you stand with Social Security, the place to start is at the website: https://www.ssa.gov/myaccount/. Think of this section as interactive. Remember, this is your retirement, so try to understand that Uncle Sam has several annoying layers of security.

Once you wade through all that, it will tell you what you are scheduled to receive depending on when you retire. That date is one of the many variables involved in retirement planning. Retire early and you get substantially less money, but over a longer period. You can start at 62, or retire out at 67 or 70. Each step boosts what you earn. (If you were born before 1960 like me, these dates vary some.)

So the first question is when you retire. It depends on how much you can afford and how long you can reasonably expect to receive the benefit. If you need the money, then retire early. It pays to wait, though, several hundred dollars more per month. As for how long you expect to receive it, don't be fooled by those life expectancy calculators that start at birth. Social Security says that:

"A man reaching age 65 today can expect to live, on average, until age 84.3."

And, "A woman turning age 65 today can expect to live, on average, until age 86.6."

If you are nearing retirement, then the odds are you have twenty to twenty-five or more years to plan for—at least. If you started work after college and worked till retirement, you are looking at funding a time lasting roughly half as long as your career.

You can't do that just on Social Security. Especially since medical expenses tend to increase as we get older.

Social Security bases its complex math on you earning for at least 35 years. Even if you maxed out every year and then retired at full retirement, it's $2,788 per month. That works out to $33,456 per year. What the average recipient gets is much lower, only about half or $16,464 per year. Depending on the cost of living where you call home, that might not be much at all. (This explains why so many seniors head south to lower-tax states.)

If you thought Social Security was going to make you rich, it's not. And if you retire before reaching full retirement, there are also limits on how much you earn.

In short, it's complicated. But it's only one part of the retirement puzzle.

I hope you are starting to realize how many inter-related parts there are to just a basic retirement. If you've spent your whole life building a business, the odds are this isn't your core competency. Why let it drag you down or sap what you've saved?

And if you want to keep your money out of Wall Street, I'm a good candidate. Remember, I'm in Midland, about as far away geographically and politically as you can be from New York.

I've been talking repeatedly about fixed-income alternatives to investing. Here's how they fit into the investment world. There are three basic categories of investing—conservative, moderate and aggressive. (Given how everything is political now, I bet you thought I was going to say "liberal.")

Conservative touches on things like CDs, government bonds, fixed annuities and even insured municipal bonds. Moderate risk includes investments like preferred stocks, corporate bonds, REITS (Real Estate Investment Trusts), master limited partnerships, business development company's and indexed annuities. The category you are most likely familiar with is the aggressive risk investments: common stocks, stock mutual funds, commodities like gold and orange juice (for you "Trading Places" fans) actual (speculative) real estate and junk bonds.

CONSERVATIVE	**MODERATE**	**AGGRESSIVE**
Certificate Of Deposit	Preferred Stock	Common Stocks
Government Bonds	Corporate Bonds	Stock Mutual Funds
Fixed Annuities	R.E.I.T.s	"Speculative" Real Estate
Insured Municipal Bonds	MLPs	
	BDCs	Junk Bonds
	Indexed Annuities	

Chart D - Source: CCG

All your life, all your training has told you to invest in the aggressive area. The business channels focus on every category there. You watch as the ticker shows the markets and then the price of top commodities: gold, silver and the West Texas favorite, oil.

You'll notice I skipped bond mutual funds off that list. I did it for a reason. They are a poor investment and not worth your time and, certainly, not worth your money. Compare buying an actual bond to a bond fund and you'll see what I mean.

When you buy a bond you get both a return on your investment when the bond matures and a fixed rate of return. When you buy a bond fund, you get neither of those.

If you were paying attention, though, I used a version of a term I've been mentioning several times in the book: "a fixed rate of return." That's what I mean by fixed-income investments. It's predictable and provides an income stream.

Investing in bonds isn't investing in bond funds. The bond might drop in value but it still pays off in the end, if you keep it till maturity. (Yes, there is a danger of a default, but that is rare.) Bonds include municipal bonds. You probably know from watching the news that cities rarely default.

There are reasons why you never hear about all this. Financial advisors recommend bond funds because they are easy and few of them specialize in or even understand the nuances of buying individual bonds. They want to play in stocks.

But there are advisors like me and others in the Advisors' Academy who understand how this works. If you find it interesting, look us up.

There's a lot more to fixed-income: preferred stocks, REITs and annuities. I'll explain later in this chapter how I used an annuity to help my Mom and ensure she had income for the rest of her life.

Each of these is complicated in its own right, depending on your tax situation. Some have tax consequences and that depends on your own tax bracket. I can't handle all the possible scenarios and you wouldn't want to take the time to read all of the possible combinations.

The point is simple: There are lots of ways to invest that provide more security and, as an added bonus, don't monopolize your time. You should own your investments. They shouldn't own you. They should provide you with security and income and help you solidify your legacy so both you and your family are safer than they would be in the market.

Investors used to care about income streams. From the 1930s to 1960s, dividends, interest rates and income were big parts of investing. Investors picked stocks that were reliable, solid companies. They weren't expected to boom or bust. They were expected to stay steady.

Then the markets really went nuts in the 1980s and 1990s. By the time we got to the dotcom crash in 2000-2001, everyone had a broker, everyone had an investment strategy. And no one was investing conservatively anymore.

And that's why the dotcom crash hurt so badly. The NASDAQ was built on tech and tech was built on greed. Who wants a bond that can provide a steady income when the stock market is going insane?

The problem with markets then, and now, is too much is based on emotion and not on core ideas. People invest because they think the stock will go up, not because they think an investment is a wise idea. They know little to nothing about the companies. All they have is the desire for a payoff.

If the mere thought of keeping your life savings in that world gives you heartburn, then you are ready for a better way of investing.

I've become militant about investing because I've heard and seen so many horror stories. Lost fortunes, disastrous investment decisions, rip-offs, con men and more. But nothing reminds you of how important all this is if you had to go through it with your own family.

When my Dad died, it was a bit of a mess. I imagine it always is. No one sets things up perfectly. And the loved ones are left sorting through files and contacts and trying to see what needs to get paid and what's left.

It all comes at a time when we are the most emotional, the most broken by circumstances. And we have no choice but to deal.

I came in late on the process. That's just how families are. Parents don't like to let go of their finances and keep control of too much information. In my case, they hadn't shared key information with me because they thought they had the time. And honestly, Great Depression people tend to be very private about the money.

The first thing we did was pay all the bills. That meant there was nothing hanging over our heads.

Fortunately, we had some property and a few things we could sell. We sold the property out in the country and paid cash for everything.

That left Mom with her Social Security and $57,000 in cash. I put $7,000 in a checking account and used the rest of the $50,000 to buy an annuity. Only Mom long outlived what they expected and she ended up getting back about $125,000 on a $50,000 investment.

After she had passed, we got a letter from the company asking her to pay back the $75,000 she had received over and above what she had paid. Since she was deceased and her estate had been settled, I wasn't legally liable for her debts. So, I sent the company a letter telling them that my Mom had passed on. And if they wanted to contact her, address it to God, care of Heaven. And if you get her on the phone, tell her I said hello.

I never heard from them again. And my mom had a nice retirement where she wasn't constantly running out of money.

Isn't that what you want, too?

DEE'S DIRECTIVES:

Do You Have The Time And Desire To Manage Your Money Every Single Day?

When my plumbing breaks, I hire a plumber. I take my car to an excellent mechanic when it starts having problems. I could probably do both those jobs if I set my mind to it. I especially enjoy cars, though today's models require computer technicians, not just gearheads.

I don't have the time. And you don't either. There are only 168 hours in a given week. Assume you sleep eight a day, though we both know you don't. Americans sleep less than seven on average and it takes a toll on our physical health. Then you work at least 40 and sometimes a lot more. Managers and small businesspeople laugh at a mere 40-hour work week. Toss in maybe an hour commuting each work day. That's already more than 100 hours. That might be a lot more for workaholics.

Now subtract out the time you spend on lunch and dinner. That's maybe two more hours a day or 14 hours total. Watch an hour of TV? That's seven more hours. Spend time on the phone talking to your kids? More time.

It's like the old expression: "Time is money." I'm a math guy. So, naturally, I assume that if two things are equal, it cuts both ways. To put it another way, that means money = time.

We spend our whole lives with this equation, deciding which is more important. When you paint your living room, you are deciding your time is less valuable than paying someone else. Plus, basic painting isn't all that tough, so it doesn't require too much expertise. Change that to painting the outside of your house in 100-degree summer heat and you are probably looking for a house painter.

You might be able to change your oil. I know a bunch of folks around Midland who like doing it. But most mechanics don't charge much for an oil change, so ordinary people prefer to pay rather than do it themselves. It saves the mess and they can focus on other, more-enjoyable things.

It's an easy equation for simple things we all understand. Mow your own lawn or pay a neighborhood teen to do it? Which is worth more to you? That all changes as the level of expertise goes up.

Our society is complicated and we lack the expertise to understand all of it. Then we hire experts. They save us time, and hassle, too.

You don't want to take on the burden of managing your finances at the same time as all your other priorities. Because, even if you do, you know it will be about 17th on your list. Your family comes first. So taking care of your financial future is also securing that future for your loved ones as well.

17.

One Piece
At A Time

NOW YOU KNOW WHAT I think about investing. What you need to figure out is how you want to handle your own finances. And you do that by learning to ask questions.

How often do you ask the right question? If you ask the wrong one, do you think you'll get the right answer? When we ask the wrong question, we never get responses that even relate to what we need to know.

What I try to teach is how to manage your finances correctly. It has to start at the very beginning, deciding on where to get your financial advice. You can go online for free and just count on what you can get on the internet. That's foolish. You won't know what's legit and what's garbage.

There's a funny expression that floats around online that's a quote from Abraham Lincoln: "The problem with internet quotes is that you can't always depend on their accuracy."[91] It's intended to be silly and to make a point that you can't trust quotes online, including this one that predates the internet by 130 years or so.

The same applies to financial advice. You can find some online. But what do you believe? The site that tells you to buy or the one that tells you to sell? Sometimes it might be the same site telling you both. Stock advisor's might recommend a stock, but the date on that recommendation could be old. You have no idea whether it's still valid or not.

Then you can pay for the advice online. Sign up with some stock-tip service. That might work, if you are a day trader. Only it depends on who gets the stock first. During the dotcom boom, stock experts like George Gilder could move the market on one recommendation. If you got it first and were able to buy, you'd make money. But if you were slow on the draw, you could lose. Tech stocks of that era were one giant roll of the dice.

Maybe you want to try handling your money yourself. You figure you've spent your life learning and earning, you'd be perfect to handle your own. I think that's a fantastic idea. How many hours a week are you going to commit? Forty? Well, that's sort of a start. I've been doing this for forty-five years. If you assume I spent just forty hours each week in that time, then I've got a bit of a leg up on you. That gives me 93,600 hours of experience.

And there's no way I spent just forty each week.

But if you want to commit the time, read dozens or hundreds of books, take courses, get licenses and expertise and then learn by doing and making mistakes along the way, go for it.

But why? To prove you can? Isn't there a mountain out there you'd rather climb? It's the same attitude and at least you'd get in shape doing it. If you are a business owner, you've spent your whole career relying on experts. Why not try one instead of killing yourself doing their job?

That takes me to financial advisors like me and many others. We vary wildly in our approaches. Some are aggressive. Some will just put you in mutual funds and expect you to ride it out. Find one who fits your goals.

And you do that by asking questions. The right questions.

Think of it like going to the doctor. You first need the right kind of specialist. If you hurt your foot, you'd never consider going to a dentist. If you need heart surgery, you wouldn't go to a dermatologist.

So you pick the right specialist for your needs. You ask around to find people you trust and hear their recommendations. You look them up online and find out something about them.

Finding a financial advisor is the same. You need to start thinking about your wealth in the same way you do your health. That old expression about being healthy, wealthy and wise didn't just happen. If you can figure out the first two, the odds are you are fairly wise.

In both cases, you hope that you found the right expert. Hope is wonderful. It makes the world go 'round. President Ronald Reagan used to have a good way of looking at problems like this. "Trust but verify," he said.

That applies here as well.

Remember, neither area is a one-size-fits-all reality. Just as your medical needs are unique to you, so too are your financial needs. Knowing the right questions to ask has to start with knowing what you want.

Asking the right questions requires the right answers. What you need for that is to find someone who sees the world the way you do. When someone comes in to meet with me, we need to learn who we are. And we do that by asking the right questions of one another.

I want them to know who Dee Carter is and what my philosophies are and what my family is like and what my background is. I don't ever turn anybody down. If they've got a problem, big or small, we're going to try to solve it. We may not be able to help them all, but I try.

I also don't want them to think I'm perfect and that I can solve any problem. I'm not Houdini. And yes, some of what I've learned, I've learned by doing the wrong way.

Financial advisors aren't perfect. One of my own financial errors was investing in an oil venture. Hey, this is West Texas. We all have to lose money on oil sometimes. In this case, it was a dry hole. I didn't ask the right questions.

I should have asked: What are the opportunities of this being a bad deal? Instead I asked: How much money can I make? I asked the wrong thing and I lost everything I put into it because I let poor decision making get the better of me. I saw dollar signs, not question marks.

I get that question all the time. What's it going to do for me? How is it going to make me money? Wrong question! And I get that a fair amount, though it used to be a lot more.

People are learning to ask the right things. Part of that is because of the internet. They Google the right questions to ask and some of what they find are useful. Not all, some. Others listen on the radio, hopefully to me. You'd better take some of what you hear on radio with a salt shaker full of salt. The good thing is, they are listening anyway and learning some of the basics. They come in here at least with some of what they heard.

Sometimes people come in here without any money. We can't fix that. We try to give them some guidance, even then.

It helps that I'm sort of a fixture here. We've been here for forty-five years and I have a lot of people that I can refer people to who can recommend me. We've never had anybody lodge a complaint against us.

It takes years to build trust. Sometimes people will just give you a try. They'll come in and put a little of their money for you to manage it and see how you do. Often a year later they tell me that they were just giving me a try.

The way to build trust is always be honest. If you can't do something, if you can't solve a problem and you don't have an answer, don't make it up off the seat of your pants. Don't come up with something that people can't live with. I think clients are sick of pie-in-the-sky promises. They'd rather have the cold, hard facts.

People learn answers by doing. Sometimes they learn by having it done to them. Financial advisors are no different.

I'm old enough to have seen a lot of market and economic disruption. I was very young, but I watched my parents endure the end of the Great Depression. And though the war ended in 1945, the markets didn't really recover until 1954. Everyone remembers the post-war boom. But the markets jumped up in 1946 and then dropped for three years. It took until 1954 just to hit the same level they had been at in 1946. And we didn't hit pre-crash levels for another five years.

I've been through several of these kinds of events. The 1987 crash. The dotcom crash and the Great Recession. Each one takes a toll on investor confidence. Clients come in with the same memories. They say, "I lost money in 2000 and again in 2007. I can't afford to do it again. I'm sixty years old. Heck, I just got back to where I was from 2008. What do I do?"

And before I can answer, they often add, "But at least I'm back even." I think, it only took you nine years to get back to square one, which means that you lost nine years of potential income, nine years of potential gain to get even, nine years to inflation, nine years of lost access to that money. And now you want to do it again?

I think not.

The questions they really want answered are: "How do I protect myself? How do I protect my life savings?"

I think when they face those decisions; we're seeing a lot more people who have gone through market disruptions—the crash of 1987, the dotcom collapse of 2000-2001 and then 2008-2009. People don't want to go through that again. And who can blame them?

They are now seeing the value of putting their money in what people did fifty years ago—fixed income investments. That's a remarkable tool, but people just kind of walked away and forgot about it. We updated it and moved it into the 21st Century, done some things that make a lot more sense for today's world.

But it's still fixed-income type products help to eliminate a large percentage of risk. The goal is so clients don't have to worry about that 2007-2009 disaster happening again.

And, let's be honest right now. We both know it's going to happen again.

We're on the cusp of big problems right now as I write this. No, that doesn't mean the market is collapsing or that you should panic when you pick up this book. But markets have cycles and one of the cycles is that they drop big time at least three times during each bear market cycle.

Dave Scranton's book "Financial Insanity" explains it very well, so I won't try to steal his thunder. I read it but I'm not one of these guys who's going to take it at face value. That meant I had my work cut out for me. I went back and started checking out his facts and figures and found that his market history back to 1899 was dead on.

When I began to study his claims, I noticed that when the market went into one of the bear secular market cycles that there were three-to-five downturns in every one of those before the market took off again.

And, almost without fail, the third time was the largest drop. (There was one case that didn't go that way. Think of it as the exception that proves the rule.) We've had two in this bear cycle we're in, since 2000. I'm sure people who don't invest know both of them by heart.

That means we're looking at the third sometime soon. We've had two drops in this secular cycle and though the market finished 2017 going great guns, I fear the old adage that what goes up must come down.

We want to put clients in a place where they can still participate in the upside of the market but limit their downside risk. That's the right thing for the customer, the right thing for our clients. And they appreciate it.

It all starts with the right questions.

I can't forget the last time we had a stock meltdown. Everywhere I went it was always the same question: "What do I do." Waiting until after a storm hits, is the wrong time to plan.

The door in my office looked like a revolving door in 2007 and 2008. We had people coming in here from every brokerage firm in West Texas, I think. The folks with money would say they had lost $200,000 or $300,000. Even the smaller clients would come in and say they had lost $10,000 or $20,000, but it seemed like $1 million to them.

The people that listened to me on the radio or heard me in my seminars and had not done anything, they suddenly decided it was important to take action.

I had been warning that it was a time to put some of their money in more conservative investments. The money they couldn't afford to lose. I said, this didn't look good. Boy that was an understatement.

We must have rolled fifty or sixty people out of the markets and into more-conservative investments. They were listening but they weren't asking the right questions. It took the market collapse to jar them into asking the right question: "What can you do for me?"

I had a client come to me in 2007 who had $1.6 million and was planning on retiring 10 years later. We talked, but he decided to leave his money in the market. Then 2008 came along and he lost a lot of money. He called me kind of frantic and said, "Can you still do what you said you can do?"

I asked him how much he had left. He told me and I said, well I still have plenty to work with. You just have less. He laughed. Then I worked with him to put the money into income-producing programs. It's not just that we doubled his money. We slashed his stress level about it. He's now retired and living the life in West Texas.

I expect the same to happen again. In 2018 or maybe 2019. When is always hard to predict. Will it happen again? I'm confident of that. And when it does, that door is going to spin like one of those old 78 rpm records. Just like it did before.

When depends on a couple things in my opinion. The real estate bubble is building in a major way as I type this. And real estate has a major market impact. There are also things that happen on the federal level that can influence markets significantly. The tax cut might slow a downturn up a bit. That will help businesses and 80 percent of taxpayers. Is it enough? I don't think so.

It took me two years to see the light on investing. I was asking the wrong questions. I had to work my way through the process. Was he right? Were his numbers accurate? It took me time to do that home-work, to ferret out the answers for myself because that's my personality.

Once I had those answers, I was able to ask the right questions. I made the decision in thirty days to move everything that I had in the business that I was doing over to Scranton. I moved it all. I've become a market evangelist. We're out here preaching a sermon that people don't want to hear because they've been hearing another version of this all their lives. Change is hard.

They've been asking the wrong questions and getting all the wrong answers all this time. Now we're trying to tell them something pro-found: Here's the question you all should be asking.

It comes with an evangelical fervor because you really want to convert people. That means to convince them about what we did for our clients, which is extremely important. I don't want my friends to lose a dime in the market. I would love for them to all come into my office and say, do what you can to protect me. Sadly, that's not going to happen. This is the real world.

I'd also love to talk to some of these young guys out there in the brokerage business and show them what I do. I want to grab them by their fancy Brooks Brother's suit collars and say: "Listen, you may be giving the wrong answers, even when your clients ask you the right questions. There's a better way of doing this."

Asking the right questions is applicable in every aspect of your life. Your spouse can't help you if you aren't communicating properly. The same goes for your plumber, your minister and every other person in your life.

We focus a lot on the front end, teaching our clients to ask those questions.

A lot of times, I'll encounter a client who seems to be dancing around a topic and not getting there—often out of fear of looking stupid. I'll smile and wait for my opening. Then I'll just say, "Let me ask the question that I think you should be asking right now." Usu-ally, when I do that, there's a huge look of relief on their faces. Then I follow up with the answer.

Now you know the questions. All you have to do is ask.

You See A Doctor For Your Health, Find An Expert For Your Wealth, Too.

Leonardo da Vinci[92] is still celebrated as the perfect example of the Renaissance man. He was an artist for the ages—both sculptor and painter. He painted The Last Supper and Mona Lisa. One of his paintings just sold for $450 million.

That career alone would carve a man in history. Except he was also a noted inventor, scientist, architect and so many other things I don't have room to list. If you are as brilliant as da Vinci, then you too can be your own expert at everything you need in life.

Except, for all his brilliance, da Vinci lived in a simpler world. He didn't have to master computers and absorb billions of words of information. That's impossible. And more impossible if you want to be good at something, so good that your life savings depends on it.

That's why I don't try to be an expert on everything. I keep in my lane. I still have an accountant to deal with the books, an electrician so I don't fry myself fixing things around the house and a parade of experts who all know their specialties. It works.

It's your turn. I've established you don't have the time to manage your finances. Now, I'm going to give you another big reason why you shouldn't do it: You probably aren't qualified. Yes, you're smart, though probably not da Vinci smart. Then again, neither am I. I know a lot of intelligent people—all with their skill sets. Few have the mindset necessary to manage their own wealth, especially for a major life change like retirement.

It's the same with your health. I'm a big fan of doctors. Especially, the wonderful Cystic Fibrosis doctors who treat my daughter Mandee. We go to doctors because we aren't as trained and experienced in medicine as they are.

Doctors endure medical school, residency and then go through years of practice perfecting their craft. We go to them to treat one of our most important assets—our bodies. Why then do people resist going to professionals to treat their financial health?

Advisors don't go to med school and, thankfully, nobody ever asked me to cut up a cadaver and perform surgery. We do, however, get licensed and spend hour after hour learning our craft and figuring the intricacies of finance.

We are your financial doctors. And just like in medicine, it's best to go for regular checkups and not wait until the patient is too sick for an expert to help. You aren't heading into retirement thinking about getting a degree in medicine to treat your various aches and pains. Why then do people think they can do the same with their equally complicated finances?

Accept it. You don't have the time to learn how to manage your finances. And there are many better things to do during retirement. That leaves you with only one viable option—take the time to hire an expert to do it properly.

Getting Ready
For Your Meeting

YOU'VE SEEN HOW SIMPLE IT IS. But before you meet with a financial advisor—me or some other professional—here are a few things you ought to know.

The people who have come to me for financial planning or retirement planning advice were often woefully misinformed as to what they could expect or what they needed to provide at that first meeting. That's why we started the pre-interviews. They help a lot with expectations.

It seems that financial advice has been thought of as almost a mystical arena and the advisor is some Merlin-esque character who sees all. Most of those who come to my office for the first time used to have little or no concept of what is about to take place.

The first thing that a potential retiree should consider is the credentials of those with whom he is discussing his or her retirement planning. How many times have you looked at the degrees on your doctor's wall? Come on, you know you have. If you see Johns Hopkins or some other big name medical institution, you breathe a quiet sigh of relief.

The same goes true here. Only don't wait till you get in the office to find out. The planner should be one who has had more than a few years of experience in the field and should be a Registered Representative of a reputable financial services company.

I would also suggest that prospective clients make sure that the advisor has completed his or her work to obtain either the Certified Financial Planner (CFP) or the Chartered Financial Planner (ChFC) designations. Those planners who have completed these areas of studies have been exposed to a gamut of planning situations and the good ones should have mastered them in order to provide a wide-range of services to their potential client.

The second thing you should consider is something that is often overlooked—chemistry. You should be comfortable with the advisor and his or her approach to retirement planning. This is a relationship built on trust. Don't work with an advisor that you can't communicate with.

Some advisors just use the products that are offered by the firms with whom they are associated and simply do not take the time to investigate the various investing opportunities that may fit the clients' best interest. Remember when I told you about asking the right questions? This is where that information really makes sense.

Some of the questions that you should be asking are:

1. How long have you been in the financial services field?
2. What is your personal attitude toward risk?
3. Do you have a financial portfolio and how has it been affected by the swings of the stock market over the past several years?
4. Are you an independent advisor or are you associated with some national firm?
5. How often can I expect to hear from you?
6. Do you have financial products that will protect my investments from the stock market, if I should choose to invest in those areas?
7. Are you growth oriented or income oriented?
8. What are your fees? How are you compensated?
9. What credentials have you earned? From what sources?
10. Will you provide me with a list of at least three of your clients that I can talk to?

A few of these questions can be answered by going to the advisor's website. Most of these will have to be answered one-on-one during your first meeting.

These are only a few questions among many that should and could be asked of a potential advisor. I try to make that easy. It has been my practice to actually provide these questions to a new client to insure that we are on the same page. I want them to have confidence in the advice that I offer to them.

If they don't ask these questions, in one form or another, I simply say, "Here are some of the questions that you did not ask of me and about which you should be concerned." Then, I ask the question for them and give them my own answers pertaining to my own practice.

I try to make sure my prospective clients have some grounding in what I do. Two of the three main groups of new clients come from areas where they've listened to my take on investing—either once or perhaps many times. They get to know me through seminars or my radio show. The third category comes from others who already know me.

I provide free educational seminars to the citizens of Midland-Odessa. I give regular talks at the local library on several different financial topics—Social Security, Basic Estate Planning Needs, Required Minimum Distributions and Year-End Tax Planning. People who attend those seminars are eager for knowledge because those topics are worrisome without it. Some of them go on to handle their own finances. A few might even hire other advisors.

I always offer those who attend our seminars a special free hour consultation. Most take advantage of it because they realize it's not going to be a hard sell. It's just another chance to have a conversation on any financial subject bothering them.

Sometimes there's an obvious rapport that comes out from those visits. Those usually result in establishing a client/advisor relationship. We ask those who take advantage of our free one-hour meeting to bring their financial paperwork with them, including their tax returns so I can answer their questions more readily. (It is amazing how many people don't realize that there are areas in their tax returns that can be turned into retirement savings if addressed properly and professionally).

We like to meet with both husband and wife, if possible, during these conversations just like standard new client meetings. That helps us understand any difference between the savings philosophy of the two of them. Some of the most hilarious and interesting things come out of these meetings.

It still amazes me that some couples who may have been married for twenty-five years or longer have never sat down and discussed financial matters. There have actually been times when I had to remove myself from my conference room to allow a couple to resolve their differences in private. As I've said before, finances are very private and no person or couple handles them the same way.

The important point of these seminars and subsequent meetings is that they don't go into their second act of life without a little coaching. Even if all they do is absorb the information I give them, they are better prepared for the future.

Roughly half of our new clients come from my weekly radio program on Midland's KWEL. They get a regular dose of me, my views on finance and the current state of the markets. It builds a base of familiarity. I think many prospective clients grow comfortable with hearing me talk finance and decide they'd like to hear more.

Listeners already feel they know me. Most of those who call for a free consultation have been listening for as long as two or three years before deciding that they need some assistance in retirement planning. When they do come in, it's almost like we're old friends, even though we've never met.

They have been listening to our philosophy of investing and their philosophies are aligned from the moment they walk in the door. We still require the same documents and tax returns, but most of these contacts are ones who are already comfortable with us and what we do. They aren't just looking for a financial solution to their problems. They know I'm skeptical of the stock market and prefer a more conservative approach. They are there because they agree.

The last group is the sign of any successful small business—client referrals. A satisfied customer makes the best reference. Sometimes that means family; friends and coworkers are recommending me to care for the finances of the people in their lives. That's the kind of recommendation people believe. I'm now assisting sons and daughters—and sometimes grandsons and granddaughters—of established clients.

These folks usually have similar needs or concerns of the referrer and already have some knowledge of what we do and how we do it. Some of them actually come in and say, "I want the same plan that my Dad (or my friend) has with you." That sounds easy, but it doesn't mean that we take any shortcuts. We still go through the same process to make sure that the person is well-suited for what we do and the products that we represent.

If a person comes in who does not fit the mold as one who is interested in retirement or deferred financial needs, we try to direct them to an area that would fit their personal needs. This isn't a generic service. This is tailored professional financial advice.

For example, I always want to know what is important about money to the prospective client. If they want to put money away for the purchase of a new car or some other item of immediate want or need, I direct them to areas of investment that will allow them to save money for that purchase. But I make sure that those who are serious about retirement planning get the necessary advice.

To sum up, don't fear meeting an advisor any more than you should fear meeting your reverend, priest or rabbi. They are there to help you, not scold you. A client should seek out an advisor they can feel comfortable talking to about any and all of their personal financial concerns.

It has to be free and honest communication. Lie and the only person you hurt is yourself. Prospective clients have to be willing to divulge mistakes they feel that they have made in the past and be willing to take the proper steps to correct these mistakes.

A good financial advisor almost becomes the client's "financial minister." The client should feel that they can talk about anything worrying them and know that, like a priest, the "confession" is private and will not be shared with anyone else.

The client should know that the advisor has the knowledge and experience to advise them in their areas of needs—whether it's budgeting, spending, saving, investing or retirement planning.

All of that has to be addressed in a professional and thoughtful manner. Financial advisors are governed by strong professional and ethical guidelines. Clients have every right to be treated honestly at all times.

And perhaps, most of all, clients should feel they can go to sleep at night and not be worried about where their money is being invested. They need to be able to rest easy that the money is as safe as it can reasonably be. And whether they live, die, become disabled or simply decide to quit what they are doing and enjoy their retirement years, what they have saved should still be there.

That is how I have been assisting my clients for many years.

And, it is a labor of love.

18.

The Ride

WE'VE ALL SEEN DOCTORS. We've been poked and prodded, injected and inspected by the best before we ever hit first grade. Going to the doctor is no big deal for most of us, even if we have what the medical field calls "white coat hypertension" or fear of going to the doctor. Like it or not, we get used to it.

Visiting a financial planner conjures up other, equally disturbing, images. The key difference is we aren't used to it. Odds are, you've never been to a financial planner. You might even think that's just for rich folks. It's not, of course. But you've never been. And you probably have awful ideas of what it's like.

I've talked to tons of clients and prospects. Many of them fear they are being taken for a ride—that somehow they've hopped into a car with a total stranger and now have absolutely no control. That scene reminded me of the popular David Allan Coe song "The Ride."

In the song, he gets picked up hitchhiking on his way to Nashville by a mysterious character. It has an ominous intro—"Now he was dressed like 1950, half drunk and hollow-eyed." Only later do we find it's the ghost of the great Hank Williams Sr., and he's giving advice to a rising young star.

The scary ride becomes a way of getting much closer to his destination. But it's still a terrifying trip.

I know that's the fear of potential clients. Even ones who know me from school or church still have similar concerns. So our practice does everything we can to cut down on the pressure and cut down on the fear.

It's not a ride. It's a conversation—between people trying to get to know one another. There's no pressure to sell and I won't even let anyone finalize things on a first meeting. I can't stand high-pressure sales tactics.

That conversation starts before a potential client ever gets in our office. We handle a pre-interview that goes over some financial basics so we have a better idea of the person's situation. Often, they don't even know. Just those questions bring them a better personal understanding of where they stand financially.

When a new potential client arrives at our office (with his or her spouse, ideally), the first thing that they notice is that the office is not "typical." Which makes sense, since neither am I. If you are looking for a stuffy Wall Street practice, then buy a plane ticket to New York.

Our office is designed to put people at ease. We have made every effort to make it more like what the clients might see in their own home. It's not all steel and glass like a set from the latest "Star Wars" movie. It's comfortable.

Sarah, our receptionist and office manager, greets them by name and invites them in. It's just as you might invite someone into your own living room. She tells them to relax and offers them soft drink, water or coffee. One of the best-known lines from our radio commercials is "we always have the coffee pot on." And we do. I don't want to put Starbucks out of business. I just want everyone to take it easy. Stressed-out people are in no place to talk about money or much of anything else.

After the visitors are seated, Sarah begins making them feel at home by telling them more about the advisor they are there to see— me. She gives them a bit of my background and that we've been in

Midland-Odessa for 45 years. She brings in my daughter Mandee, our client service specialist, and explains how this is a family business.

I find that helps make people feel at home. They aren't dealing with a company based out of a city 1,800 miles away. They are dealing with a business whose owner lives nearby, maybe shops at the same stores as them, goes to the same restaurants and knows more about their background. After a few minutes, Sarah brings them into my office.

Whatever they are expecting, this probably isn't it. My office is unusual, to say the least. It looks more like the Kiwanis Club sponsored by an Elvis convention—resulting in an eclectic mix of memorabilia lining the walls and shelves. There are two guitars hanging just opposite my desk as they walk in. Those are joined by that incredible original pastel picture of Elvis Presley I described earlier.

Talk about conversation starters.

Most folks in West Texas know that I spent several years working as an Elvis Presley tribute artist. They might even have heard me perform. And if they are Elvis fans (and who isn't?), they want to know about the picture and the Elvis guitar. I am always happy to share a few brief stories about my "Elvis years," if the new client wants to talk about it. I think it helps seeing me as a real person with interests outside of work. The visit just naturally turns into a friendly conversation.

As soon as I can feel that we've broken the ice, I invite them to join me in my private conference room. I want to get away from the desk as soon as I can because I feel that it is a barrier between me and the client. I want them to feel totally at ease prior to getting into the "meat" of the meeting.

We shift gradually into the important topics. I first ask about their family and their jobs. A financial advisor often takes on that role not just for the client, but to oversee money intended to send children to college or care for an ailing family member.

It helps to know how many children they have, whether they have boys or girls or both and how old their children are. We discuss their work and how long they have been with their current employer. The same goes for their spouse.

My roots are deep in the dusty soil of West Texas. I am usually familiar with the company either from the information that they have already supplied or because I've been in business in Midland for more than 45 years with now more than 800 clients, odds are I know someone else who works at the same company, perhaps even the owner. Midland-Odessa has many of the benefits of a good-sized city, but it is still a small town at heart.

After a few minutes discussing personal history (marriage, education, etc.) we get to the key part of the meeting. And I always start it off the same. My first question is, "What concerns bring you to our office today?"

I have never had anyone pause before they began to answer my question. Depending on what they envision their concerns to be, I know exactly where to go from there. There's no jumping to sales talk or trying to get them to sign on the line that is dotted.

My job is simple. I'm there to listen to their concerns and make sure that they have a clear picture in their mind what their financial concerns are. Then and only then, are they are prepared to take the necessary steps to solve those problems.

The answers are seldom the same, but they stopped surprising me a couple decades ago. They usually want to know about retirement. It's ominous. You spend your whole life working and it becomes a huge piece of our identity. Retiring is like being reborn and we all have questions.

Others worry about their legacy or how to take care of children or sick family members. The questions come sometimes like a drizzle and other times like a monsoon. I'm there to answer.

That's the part of the process when I smooth over their worries. We talk out issues. Sometimes there may be family members who are in the insurance and financial services business. People are private about their money. Most want to see a professional financial advisor who isn't in the family for privacy as well as professional distance. Clients don't want an advisor who knows them so well that they never hear the truth.

It's similar when people are seeking a doctor or attorney and they'd rather find one outside the family. People are just more comfortable sharing personal information with someone who isn't related.

If the pre-interview worked properly, and it usually does, the new client has brought some fundamental paperwork along. That might include IRAs, an old 401(k) account that has never been rolled over, CDs and checking account statements, quarterly reports from their current advisor or tax returns. Sometimes it's all of the above and more. That helps us size up the situation from a financial standpoint.

We walk through that a bit just so I understand the basics. I need to know enough so I can help.

Then we begin to wind things down. No recommendations are made at the first visit. That's a firm rule. By sticking to it, I remove any doubt from the clients. They can leave and no one will twist their arm on the way out.

Our initial goals are always the same: Make the client feel comfortable with us and our process and feel comfortable sharing their financial situation with us. If we've managed this, it's a win for everyone, even if they choose to look elsewhere. I know that somehow I've helped.

Once this has been discussed, it is very easy to set a second appointment. That gives me a chance to review their financial picture and come up with some suggested solutions. The interim also gives them an opportunity to decide if they like the idea of working with me. The initial impression sinks in and, typically, they are eager to come back.

The first meeting usually lasts for one to one-and-a-half hours. That's about as long as you'd take for lunch. Sometimes things run a bit longer, depending on how much material is supplied by the client. We hope to get them back for a second meeting within a week while the information is still fresh.

That's the easy part. The next piece of the puzzle comes when I work through their finances and assess what I think is the best approach. I do a thorough evaluation of their financial information and I search among the companies that I represent for the very best answer possible. I'm looking for investments that I think best fit their needs and pain threshold. I'm not out to make money for financial companies.

I was asked by one of the strongest annuity companies in the country to appear at their March 2018, agents' forum, though I'm sure that event is long past if you are reading this. They wanted me to speak to several hundred of their top representatives about how advisors work with their firm. The topic I was asked to cover was, "How do you direct your clientele to choose our company for their retirement partner?"

I chuckled when I was asked about that. My answer to the vice president who had invited me to speak at the meeting was short and sweet. "I don't!" Once he was able to control his surprised expression, he said, "But you are one of our top representatives and you say you don't direct your clients to our company?"

My reply caught him by surprise, but it is one of my essential beliefs. "As long as you have the best retirement contract in the industry, you will be receiving my business. But, if the time ever comes that another company is better for the needs of my clientele, the money will be going there." I got the feeling no one had ever told him that before.

It's easy to lose sight of who you work for—clients or the financial companies. I feel an immense responsibility to make sure that the people who walk out of my door as new clients have the best product available for their particular needs. I believe this one core belief is the main reason that I am still in business in Midland, for over 45 years.

I'm sure the new clients understand it. After our first meeting, the client is comfortable with my procedures and knows, beyond a doubt, that whatever solution I bring to the table will address their problem and put them on the road toward financial success.

The second meeting is more of an education. I summarize their concerns and, step by step, provide our solutions. After I lay everything out, I always ask a simple question, "Where do we go from here?"

The answer is almost always the same: "Where do you think we should go?" My response is, "Are you asking me as someone who will be working with you to solve these problems?" That's as low pressure as I can make it.

When they respond affirmatively, we work on filling out any necessary paperwork to move their funds into the right places to solve their problems. The paperwork is essential and I have my daughter Mandee, specialize in helping the clients filling out of the forms.

It's friendly and relaxed. This isn't taking anyone for a ride, but they arrive at their destination nonetheless.

I try to see four to five clients a day, at least four days a week. That can mean long days, depending on the number of people calling for appointments. A lot of that is market driven and in good (or bad) market weeks I find myself still at the office late and working all day Friday as well.

You know what? I don't mind at all. When that happens I know I am able to help more people. I love what I do. Seeing those people relax and realize that they can go to bed at night and rest easier is a great reward for me. It's a great life. I am able to work at a job that I love and know that the client will always benefit more from the relationship, money-wise, than I ever will.

DEE'S DIRECTIVES:

Find An Advisor Who Will Tell You The Truth, Even The Hard Truth.

I'm hoping I've convinced you. I've been building the case for 18 chapters about how you need a professional financial advisor—especially heading into your retirement. I've made the case that you don't have the time or expertise. And now I've tried to explain to you the questions necessary to choose the best advisor for you.

There's a key component of that choice that doesn't get much attention. Part of it is because it sounds so basic—telling the truth.

Telling the truth should be easy, but it's not. The philosopher Diogenes used to carry a lamp claiming he was looking for an honest man. He'd have a hard time in the modern world. Politicians lie constantly. Marketers exaggerate the truth just as often. And on down the line.

Sometimes people lie because they don't think we want the truth. In the words of Jack Nicholson from "A Few Good Men," "You can't handle the truth!" He was right. We can't. We want our loved ones to spare our feelings and doctors to give bad news to us gently.

That's garbage. And you deserve better than garbage. You need a financial advisor who will tell you the truth. If you are throwing your money into a bad investment, you want him or her to stop you. If you aren't saving enough for your retirement, you need to hear about it.

This isn't just the financial version of bedside manner. I'm not suggesting you find an advisor to tell you that you're an idiot. That individual wouldn't be in business very long. This is different. It's a doctor's job to tell you to eat better, or sleep more. And it's a financial advisor's role to be responsible for telling you how to save more or invest more wisely.

That's especially difficult given how much media we are all bombarded by. Most advisors would back down from customers who want to be 100 percent in high-risk stocks, even if that's not wise for their time in life. Sure, they might say that's not ideal. But they'd generally prefer keeping a client happy over saying what needs to be said.

That's not who I am. And that's not the kind of expert you need to hire. You wouldn't want an electrician to tell you it's OK to overload a circuit. And you don't want a financial expert to let you risk your future. This is why I switched how I managed money for my clients. The old way was tearing me up, costing me my sleep and my health.

I've been preaching a new, more-conservative way of investing because it works and gives you more peace of mind. You need the kind of advisor who will give you an honest assessment of your finances, not blow smoke. Listen to them!

19.

My Way

I'VE HAD A WONDERFUL life. I think of myself as Jimmy Stewart in the movie of a similar name. Only I'm not the bitter, depressed Jimmy at the beginning of the film. I'm the Frank Capra success story. I'm the Jimmy at the end of the film surrounded by friends and family and perfectly happy in his life, perfectly happy in the community that has been such a part of that life.

I have a wife who loves me and is good-hearted and strong-willed enough to keep me in check. Four amazing kids, three incredible grandchildren. I've played music with some of the best both rock and country had to offer. I've travelled the world, performed as Elvis and even competed on a national stage with the best. I've been part of a group that sang at the Vatican. I've met presidents and senators, businessmen and church leaders.

I've even met The King.

My faith has helped guide me on every bit of that path—both when I stayed on it and when I strayed. It helped me find the heart to give—to help others, to aid my church and to fund the alma mater

I love so much. As I quoted my favorite hymn earlier, "It is well with my soul."

I'm proud of all of that. But I'm just as proud of my professional legacy, of the business I built and of the people I helped—first in faith and later in finances.

I don't worship money. I love having it not for the Midas-like thrill of accumulation. I love it because money lets us do what we want, help who we want and care for those who mean the most to us. Money is simply a means to an end.

As I get a bit nearer to that end, that becomes clearer. No, this isn't a final testament. God's going to have to drag me out of this life. I like it here too much. But reaching three quarters of a century gives one perspective.

It also means I'm a bit different from every group I meet.

I went to a men's retreat some time back and the minister there asked if I'd mind saying a few words. You know me by now. That's like asking Dracula if he wants some blood. So, of course, I said yes. Then I thought for a second and asked why. I got the answer I didn't want to hear, because I was the oldest there.

I get that answer a lot now.

There were seventy men there and I was the oldest. In nearly every crowd I'm in, I'm the oldest guy there. But I don't care how old I am as long as I am one year older next year.

I stood up and took a look around the room. I reached into my heart for the words, realizing that I was supposed to come up with some finely aged wisdom. I said to them, "Guys, I have run the race." As I said it, I could feel it, picture it.

There I was, the younger me. You know, the one you picture when you think of yourself and when Father Time isn't staring back at you from that dreadful mirror. I imagined myself at a starting block, maybe eighteen or nineteen years old. I took off and nothing could stop me. There's a huge crowd, hundreds, maybe thousands of other racers of all sizes, shapes and colors running with me. Some fall out of the pack. At first, it's one or two. Then dozens. I could feel myself moving slower and I looked at the other racers who were still running and they're aging, so I figured I must be as well.

In the distance, I can see a finish line. It's hard to know how far yet, but I can see it. And I am determined to get there.

As that flashed through my mind, I continued. "I know I'm on the home stretch. I can see the tape from here. That might be 20 years from now, but I can see it."

This book is the way to run through the tape.

That's what we all need to do, run through the tape. Live every moment like you are still competing, still striving, up to the final moment. Keep on running until you can't.

That's easier for me than many people. Some people when they get older become Eeyores,[93] from "Winnie the Pooh"—stubborn and unhappy. I'm a Tigger. I'm a ball of energy, full of bounce and optimism and I plan on staying that way.

Since my business is one of my points of pride and accomplishment, it's essential to me that I pass things along slowly to the next generation. And that's what I'm planning to do, to gradually bring my daughter Mandee along so she learns the ins and outs of the business, until she can take over when I'm gone.

Many family owned businesses fail in that transition and I won't have it. Mandee is family, but my clients are like family. It's important that she know all she needs to know before they come and drag me out of here.

And, God willing, that won't be soon. Whenever she finds me dead at my desk is when she can take over. Not one second sooner. So she has plenty of time to learn and master this.

It won't be easy. Leadership transitions seldom are—in politics, in sports and in business. It's going to force us to expand our relationship. So when she walks through that door, she takes on a different mindset. I'm Daddy outside that door and I don't want that to change ever. Inside that door, it's an office and it's professional.

I will not walk away from helping people until I either cannot do it or just don't want to anymore. And I can't see that scenario ever happening. I enjoy it too much. I enjoy helping my flock too much. It's not a job to me and it really never has been. It's a calling.

One of the most difficult things in any kind of business is passing the torch, especially if you're passing it to a close family member. It's not quite so difficult to pass it to someone else, because you really can say things and teach in ways that would harm that familial relationship.

It's a challenge on both sides. We both need to walk a fine line. I need to educate her, support her when she's learning, celebrate her victories and counsel her defeats. That's where I become more of a boss and less of a dad.

It's just as difficult for her. She has made a decision this is what she wants to do. She knows that's a commitment and it comes with all sorts of obligations. She has to be afraid of letting me down both as an employee and as a daughter.

But we both know there's no failing in this. If we fail, we let each other down. But more importantly, we let our clients down. And we can't, we won't let that happen.

In so many ways, Mandee is just like me. She's done several types of jobs refining her craft, including both administrative work and sales.

She's vivacious and has an incredible personality. But what makes her truly incredible is all she has overcome in her life. That's why I know she'll be able to take over for me. Because there's no obstacle she can't overcome.

The result is she's both ambitious and sensitive. Part of that is because she's been fighting Cystic Fibrosis since she was seven. Fighting and winning. That whole time she was told that she probably wouldn't even live a normal lifetime. It makes you strong. Now, thanks to medical science, she's taking medication that should extend her life to a normal span.

That means, decades from now, she'll be the one they have to drag out of this office.

When we first found out about the CF, Susan and I both just lost it. It's so hard for parents to watch their little ones get sick and not be able to help. That meant I did the only thing I could do. I prayed.

Every day for twenty-five years, I would start my day with my little devotional. And every prayer was always the same: "God, please find a way to make Mandee well." Twenty-five years later, scientists came up with this wonder drug called Kalydeco.[94]

Mandee and Susan were actually in Dallas seeing her CF doctor at the Southwest Medical Center. While they were there, I saw on TV that this drug had been developed that covered just four percent of the people with the problem. Just four percent. I called Susan and told her.

Susan's voice was strained. She tried to laugh and said, "That's funny. We've been crying for the last hour. Dr. Raksha Jain, Mandee's CF specialist, told us that she was one of the four percent." I just sat there in my house and cried and thanked God.

CF is one of those things that is so awful, it's hard for families to even talk about. I can have a heart-to-heart with Mandee about just about anything. This was always too tough for us. One of the ways I handled it was always donating whatever I could to research to overcome this hideous problem. I did a lot of my Elvis performing that way, donating my part of the proceeds to the CF Foundation.

There's one of those times that always sticks with me when I think of Mandee.

When I used to do those shows, I would break them into two parts. The first half would be gospel. It was complete with me wearing my white Elvis suit, and I had this marvelous sixteen-person gospel group as backup. And then second half was going to be a '70s Elvis revue.

This particular time, we gave tickets away to all the families who had Cystic Fibrosis children. There must have been twenty to twenty-five families there.

The concert began and the backup singers and this outstanding band are on stage, building up the momentum for the crowd. I'm off stage singing with a cordless mic and then I walk on stage as Elvis. I think the white suit got a standing ovation.

At the half, I went back to change into my jumpsuit. That left

Mandee on the stage with our emcee Bill Warren, who was a local TV personality. I didn't think anything of it, until he started talking to her—in front of the audience.

He interviewed her about her CF. He was asking questions I never had the courage to ask her. It was the first time I ever heard Mandee really talking about it. Here she is on stage in front of hundreds of people and she is opening up about the problems, not just her problems, but the problems for everyone who has CF.

There were probably twenty-five or thirty children in the audience who had CF just like her. They knew. Her nightmare was theirs. Her troubles, her strength spoke to and for every child there.

I was standing right behind her, but hidden behind the curtain. Tears were streaming down my face as I heard her talk about the challenges she faced. I was so wiped out, I had to go outside to compose myself so I could sing again.

She wasn't telling the audience about her weakness or her disease. She was telling the audience about how it made her strong, about what she had to overcome and how she, and those twenty-five children, all were overcoming it.

That's why I know she can do anything she sets her mind to.

I still have no illusions that the transition will be easy. Nothing worthwhile ever is. It's difficult to communicate to a family member the importance of doing the same thing you've been doing for years. Mandee doesn't come from the same generation with the same attitudes. Her generation does things differently. In fact, doing things differently is one of their strengths. They're more tech savvy, which is wonderful. But that isn't a replacement for knowledge. It's just a tool.

Mandee has a caretaker personality and you absolutely need that in this job. You have to be a caretaker, not just a taker. You need to care for your clients like they're your own kin. Now, I raised her as a good Christian and she doesn't have to be shown what's right and wrong. That's innate for her and it's another key. Ethics is another essential in this business. They can be no cutting corners on it, either. Reputations are built over years and destroyed overnight.

There are three things I think she'll need to do, but that apply to anyone taking over a family business.

The No. 1 rule is to communicate to anyone taking over that they need to do the things that have to be done a certain way—the way you want and the way the clients demand. There are reasons why things are done. Sometimes it's just comfort zone of the client and sometimes there are either legal or financial reasons for what we do. There are a lot of both in this business.

The second rule is learning what you need to learn in order to handle the job. There's a ton of learning in financial planning. We never stop, so she'll be in school or taking classes the rest of her life. There's two ways to do that learning in financial planning—watching and reading. She has to do both. Mandee has to do that learning so she can figure out the right questions to ask and how to lead a client to asking the right ones back.

That part of the process is going great. Mandee already does some of the work in the office while she learns. She also she sits in on my interviews. That's the watching part of education. One day, I threw her a curve. I told her: "Mandee, why don't you start this one out on your own." I got up and walked out of the room. She looked at me funny at first, but didn't miss a beat. She did well and made both her boss and her Dad proud.

I came back in several minutes later and took over as things got a little more complicated. But I was listening the whole time, observing how much she had already gleaned from watching me. It was a good beginning. I had mentors do the same for me in my career. Now, I've shifted my role a bit so I'm not a Dad 24-7. Some of the time, I'm her mentor.

The third rule is the toughest for the younger generation. It's having the dedication to get the job done. It sounds basic, but work is hard. Sometimes you just need to apply more hours to a problem to keep moving forward. I've met some millennials who won't do that.

I'm not sure that's something you can teach. It's something you have to want to learn. Mandee has watched me be my workaholic self all her life. She's smart, so there's no question that she knows what has to be done.

She's great in reading people and majored in psychology, which is a huge part of this job. Learning what the client wants and needs is essential. I think in some ways, her background is pretty similar to mine. Instead of financial backgrounds, we both have people backgrounds. And this is a people business.

But it's still a business and running a business well, especially a small business, you learn that by going to the School of Hard Knocks. I've met MBA experts who were great at finance but couldn't run a hot dog stand. And they didn't have the desire to learn.

That's an entirely separate set of skills I have to teach—managing clients and managing staff are totally different. Handling customer accounts and making sure the bills get paid are different, too. That doesn't come quickly. It's harder to teach than financial planning.

Over time, she'll learn everything I do working with clients, she'll master everything from the first interview to presentations and events. Mandee will get so steeped in this knowledge that she'll be dreaming financial planning. And when we finally get to that point, I'll step back from that part of the business.

To get to that point, she'll be going to training through the Advisors' Academy[95]. I go to at least one a year because Dave can use me as an example. She'll go and absorb a ton of what she needs to know. But this will work better with both of us there, going through the lessons together.

The next step is no fun for her, but I'll love it. She'll have to start doing the paperwork and I'll be checking it. There's a mountain of paperwork in financial planning. I want her to learn how to fill out every single document. I'm literally going to stop filling out a single page.

She'll get to a point where she graduates a bit and works with a client from A all the way to Z, with me just sitting there observing. Once she can do that, she's off to the races. We'll start getting her licenses. In Texas, she can get temporary insurance for six months as long as she's being mentored by someone and that's obviously me. That gives her six months to learn and for her to take her test. The test isn't that hard if you study a lot. It's a hundred and fifty questions and most people pass the first time. She'll need to study and pass the Series 65 exam as well.

She has lots of studying to do.

I'll still be involved in running the whole operation. Because that's a separate skill set. I've spent decades mastering that. It's why my business is still standing after several boom-and-bust cycles here in West Texas.

I do have a plan. A plan for my business, a plan to keep on enjoying every second God gives me on this earth, a plan to keep being thankful and helping others. A plan to try to be the best man I can be, even though I know I will fail every single time. Because we are human and we are never perfect.

I have a plan. Now it's your turn.

DEE'S DIRECTIVES:

Your Legacy.

Matthew 5:12 says: "Rejoice and be glad, for your reward in heaven is great." Let me add, but your time on earth is limited. Advisors dance around this topic because it makes people uncomfortable. Our time on earth is temporary. We all know it. We just hate to admit it.

There's a huge difference between knowing it and doing something about it. It's time you took the second step. This whole book is about preparing for your future. The only responsible thing to do is to include preparing for death, as well.

Yes, I just typed the dreaded "D" word. I know people in both finance and ministry who avoid using it. It's too jarring, they say. No, it's just reality. It used to be more of a common aspect of all of our lives. Families were closer and people didn't live anywhere near as long. We learned to cope with their passing when we were young.

It's a serious topic and, thankfully, you still have a chance to address it. You have a chance to make sure things are handled responsibly so they can put your family and your loved ones in the best-possible position. There are several ways to do this.

The first is life insurance. You might have a policy through your employer, but what happens when you retire? Funerals are expensive and a policy can help with those costs. Your family will also have to cope with the loss of your income. A good life insurance policy can help there, also.

Then there's full-on estate planning. That ends up being a mixture of organizational and financial. You need a Will at bare minimum. That means you will need to designate an executor of your estate— someone you trust to be fair and responsible.

You will need to figure out how you want your estate divided. This should be simple if you are married, with everything going to your spouse. Perhaps a few personal items might be passed on to family or friends. This takes on more importance if you don't have direct heirs—like a spouse or children.

A proper estate attorney will help you sort through all of this. They typically have tip sheets for you to designate your most-important possessions. It still falls on your shoulders. What you consider important might not be the most valuable. A treasured ring or an album of family photos might be worth more to you than your 401(k). The question you have to ask yourself is who in the family would treat them the same.

An estate attorney will also get into the medical side of things and that can vary from state to state. Living wills and healthcare power of attorney are essential tools so you know your wishes will be carried out. It's also a must to make your wishes clear to your family. Some doctors will defer to the wishes of the family if you can't speak for yourself.

The goal is simple: You want to make sure that your estate is handled the way you want it after you are gone. But there's a lot more to your legacy than that. Money, the money you have saved throughout decades of your working life, is an essential piece of that legacy.

It isn't your whole legacy. Don't get confused. Sure, those dollars can go to securing your family's future and aiding the charities that matter to you. I've spent my career helping people with their finances so they could live the lives they wanted.

Hopefully, this book will help you secure your financial health. It's designed to give you some of the tools you'd get if you hired a professional financial advisor like me. We help you stabilize your life, so that money becomes one of your smaller worries. If you become extremely wealthy maybe America will remember you for what you gave away. Maybe you can be another Andrew Carnegie.

Personally, I'd rather be remembered for more than that. Be remembered for every life you touch—your spouse and your children for starters. Your friends and coworkers matter as well. The people you help when you volunteer at church or work that soup kitchen line. The strangers that you aid and the good will you pass along. Every life you encounter in person, and even online, is one you can make better.

All that is your legacy, too, your mark on this place called earth. Live every day like you want people to remember you for what you did just that day. That's your legacy.

I've had a great time at life, making my mark and leaving my own legacy. There are few thrills like the roar of a crowd when you come on stage or the standing ovation when that same crowd loves you. It's easy to see how entertainers become addicted to it. Except that pales in comparison to holding the tiny body of your newborn baby girl. The joys of family outweigh every second I ever spent singing and I adore singing.

I've seen the world or at least a lot of it. Toured America and loved every nook and cranny. I've seen many of the sights of the Old World that make the tour books and, sometimes, the history books.

And I've had fun doing it all. Maybe singing isn't your thing and, honestly, I doubt many of my readers want to perform like Elvis. But there are things *you* like to do that never get the time and attention you want.

Do them. Make time for the things you enjoy. That's why you've worked so hard. That's why you've saved so much. If you've always wanted to go on safari in Africa and see elephants in the wild, then go while you still can. Want to ski the Swiss Alps? Save for it, just pack some warm clothes. Take the time out of your busy schedule and go. Be sure to have fun.

Enjoy your life. It's the only one you get on this earth.

20.

Afterword

WHERE IS DEE NOW? Dee Carter can be found on any day in his office in Midland, Texas at the Carter Financial Group. That is, if he isn't out and about on his radio show or helping his community by doing one of a hundred different philanthropic "passions" for his church or his family and friends (and that's quite a large group of people).

To learn more about Dee and what he is doing, or maybe to get to know Mandee (his daughter and partner) or Dee on a personal basis—or if you have questions you would like for them to answer about this book—please go to (https://carterfinancial.fixedincomecounsel.com/about-us/our-people/) or call (432) 685-1372) and schedule an appointment.

Dee can be found doing his radio show every Monday morning at 8:00 am on KWEL, AM 1070, FM 107.1 on your dial—dispensing his wisdom with humor and grace—which is why his program is listened to from Texas to Ft. Lauderdale and back again.

As the publisher of this book I can honestly say that Dee is a pleasure to get to know, whether as a friend, business associate or trusted financial advisor. Please familiarize yourself with his website and radio show where he dispenses solid advice each and every day.

If you are of retirement age, not only will Dee impress upon you that "it's now or never" but if I may extend just one more old fashioned saying, because in today's world of disappearing values; where real men are a dwindling resource, Dee Carter is "one in a million."

Michelle OHalloran
Partner, Advisors Academy Press

NOTES

CHAPTER ONE

1. OCS: OfficeXCommissioned Officers are the managers, problem solvers, key influencers and planners who lead Enlisted Soldiers in all situations. Candidate School (OCSXOfficer Candidate School allows college graduates to gain the knowledge and skills necessary to be commissioned as an Army Officer.) is the U.S. Army's main training academy for prospective Army Officers.XCommissioned Officers are the managers, problem solvers, key influencers and planners who lead Enlisted Soldiers in all situations. The school is generally open to qualified enlistedXEnlisted Soldiers perform specific job functions and have the knowledge that ensures the success of their unit's current mission within the Army. Noncommissioned Officers,XCommissioned Officers are the managers, problem solvers, key influencers and planners who lead Enlisted Soldiers in all situations. along with civilians who hold at least a four-year college degree. https://www.goarmy.com/ocs.html

2. Nordenham: Is located on the West Bank of the Weser River across from Bremerhaven along the river's mouth at the North Sea, north of the cities of Bremen and Oldenburg. https://en.wikipedia.org/wiki/Nordenham

3. Obersalzberg: Is a mountainside retreat situated above the market town of Berchtesgaden in Bavaria, Germany. Located about 120 kilometers (75 mi) southeast of Munich. https://en.wikipedia.org/wiki/Obersalzberg

CHAPTER TWO

4. Texicans: Also used Texians, were residents of Mexican Texas and, later, the Republic of Texas. Today, the term is used specifically to distinguish early Anglo settlers of Texas. https://en.wikipedia.org/wiki/Texians

5. Franklin D. Roosevelt our 32nd President (1933-1945): https://www.whitehouse.gov/about-the-white-house/presidents/franklin-d-roosevelt/

6. Monahans: Is a city in and the county seat of Ward County, Texas, United States. A very small portion of the city extends into Winkler County.: https://en.wikipedia.org/wiki/Monahans, Texas

CHAPTER THREE

7. ROTC Reserve Officers Training Corps: https://www.goarmy.com/rotc

NOTES

CHAPTER FOUR

8. The Rainy Day by Henry Wadsworth Longfellow: http://www.hwlongfellow.org/poems_poem.php?pid=39
9. Morton Frozen Foods: Is the brand name of a now-discontinued line of frozen foods, including honey buns, jelly donuts, and pot pies. http://www.brandlandusa.com/2015/08/10/history-of-morton-frozen-foods-part-1/
10. Adulting: To do grown up things. https://www.merriamwebster.com/words-at-play/adulting
11. Abilene Christian University: https://grad.acu.edu/about.php
12. Southbound 35: A Pat Green Album, Dancehall Dreamers Released: 1995 https://en.wikipedia.org/wiki/Pat_Green

CHAPTER FIVE

13. Cenotaph: A tomb or a monument erected in honor of a person or group of persons whose remains are elsewhere. https://www.merriam-webster.com/dictionary/cenotaph
14. Average U.S. Household Debt Department of the Treasury: http://www.foxnews.com/politics/2012/10/02/federal-deficit-increased-by-13-trillion-in-fiscal-2012.html

CHAPTER SIX

15. Total U.S. Household Debt 13 Trillion: https://www.forbes.com/sites/zackfriedman/2017/11/14/debt-auto-loans/#19737b24ffbf
16. "That's All Right": Is a song written and originally performed by blues singer Arthur Crudup, March 1949. The Elvis Presley version of this song was released on Sun labels, July 1954. https://www.elvisrecords.com/sun-thats-all-right-blue-moon-of-kentucky/
17. Walk The Line: "Recorded in April 1956, Cash's first #1 was sped up at the urging of Sun Studios owners Sam Phillips." http://www.songfacts.com/detail.php?id=5936
18. Hey Miss Fannie: Roy Orbison went to Dallas, TX to record "Ooby Dooby" and "Hey, Miss Fannie" which appears to be a duet of Roy and James Morrow. The session took place at some point during the summer of 1955 before the boys returned to West Texas. Roy was convinced that they would be signed to Columbia Records, which never happened. https://www.sunrecords.com/artists/roy-orbison
19. KMID: KMID-TV Channel 2, Midland TX https://www.sunrecords.com/artists/roy-orbison
20. Tom Dooley: The Story of Tom (Dula) Dooley. http://ncvisitorcenter.com/Story_of_Tom_Dooley.html

21. Where Have All The Flowers Gone: The melody and the first three verses were written by Pete Seeger in 1955 and published in *Sing Out!* Magazine. Peter, Paul and Mary included the song on their eponymous debut album (which spent five weeks as the #1 album in the country) in 1962. https://en.wikipedia.org/wiki/Where_Have_All_the_Flowers_Gone%3F

22. Jack Daniels Carlson: Founded Highway 101 in 1986 in Los Angeles, California, with guitarist Jack Daniels, bassist Curtis Stone (son of singer Cliffie Stone) and drummer Scott "Cactus" Moser, all three of whom were session musicians.[3] Carlson and Daniels returned in 1996 for the album *Reunited*, released via Intersound Records. "Where'd You Get Your Cheatin' From" and "It Must Be Love" were released as singles. In 1998, Carlson and Daniels would both depart Highway 101 once again.

23. Emmy Lou Harris: Born April 2, 1947 in Birmingham, Alabama Is an American singer, songwriter and musician. She has released many popular albums and singles over the course of her career, and she has won 13 Grammys as well as numerous other awards, including induction into the Country Music Hall of Fame. http://www.emmylouharris.com/

24. Morris Mac Davis (born January 21, 1942): Is a country music singer, songwriter, and actor, originally from Lubbock, Texas, who has enjoyed much crossover success.
    Mac Davis's "Texas in my Rear View Mirror" was a #9 Country Music Hit in 1980. It was released on the Casablanca Records LP at the end of 1980. https://en.wikipedia.org/wiki/Mac_Davis

25. Barbara Ann Mandrell (born December 25, 1948): Is an American country music singer, musician, and actress. http://www.imdb.com/name/nm0005178/bio

26. Hee Haw: Welcome to Kornfield Kounty & HEE HAW! SA-LUTE! Hee Haw, a country version of Rowan and Martin's Laugh In, was a staple of syndicated television for more than 20 years. It began as a weekly series on CBS in 1969, but the network canceled it in 1971 as part of an attempt to cleanse its schedule of rural-flavored shows (other casualties included The Beverly Hillbillies and Green Acres). http://www.tv.com/shows/hee-haw/

27. Dow Jones Industrial Average: Peaks in October of 2007 (Bear Market of 2007 To 2009) https://en.wikipedia.org/wiki/United_States_bear_market_of_2007%E2%80%9309

CHAPTER SEVEN

28. The King Elvis Aaron Presley: Was born to Vernon and Gladys Presley in a two-room house in Tupelo, Mississippi, on January 8, 1935. http://www.elvis.com/about/bio

29. Fluffernutter: A fluffernutter is a sandwich made with peanut butter and marshmallow fluff usually served on white bread. https://en.wikipedia.org/wiki/Fluffernutter

30. Montreux, Switzerland: The town of Montreux nestles in a sheltered Lake Geneva bay, surrounded by vineyards and against the breathtaking backdrop of snow-covered Alps. https://www.myswitzerland.com/en-us/montreux.html.

31. Honor Flight Honor Flight Network: Is a non-profit organization created solely to honor America's veterans for all their sacrifices. We transport our heroes to Washington, D.C. to visit and reflect at their memorials. Top priority is given to the senior veterans—World War II survivors, along with those other veterans who may be terminally ill. https://www.honor-flight.org/

CHAPTER EIGHT

32. The Areopagus or Mars Hill: Is a bare marble hill next to the Acropolis in Athens. It is especially popular with travelers for its connections with a speech made by Paul the Apostle. http://www.sacred-destinations.com/greece/athens-areopagus-mars-hill

33. Gstaad, Switzerland: Is a village in the German-speaking section of the Canton of Bern in southwestern Switzerland. https://en.wikipedia.org/wiki/Gstaad

34. Sachsenhausen: 1936-1945 The Sachsenhausen Concentration Camp was built in the summer of 1936 by concentration camp prisoners from the Emsland camps. http://www.stiftung-bg.de/gums/en/

35. Midland-Odessa Symphony & Chorale: Under the baton of Music Director & Conductor Gary Lewis, the Midland-Odessa Symphony & Chorale (MOSC) is enriching lives through music in Midland, Odessa and the surrounding areas. Unique, compared to similar orchestras throughout the United States, the Midland-Odessa Symphony & Chorale includes a symphony orchestra, a chorale and a youth choir along with three resident instrumental ensembles. http://www.mosc.org/about/

36. Saint Francis: Founder of the Franciscan Order, born at Assisi in Umbria, in 1181. http://www.catholic.org/saints/saint.php?saint_id=50

37. Cattedrale di Santa Maria del Fiore Santa Maria del Fiore: Designed by Arnolfo di Cambio, is the third largest church in the world (after St. Peter's in Rome and St. Paul's in London) and was the largest church in Europe when it was completed in the 15th century. It is 153 meters long, 90 meters wide at the crossing, and 90 meters high from the floor to the bottom of the lantern. The third and last cathedral of Florence, it was dedicated to Santa Maria del Fiore, the Virgin of the Flower, in 1412, a clear allusion to the lily, the symbol of the city of Florence. It was built over the second cathedral, which early Christian Florence had dedicated to St. Reparata. https://www.museumflorence.com/monuments/1-cathedral

38. Kauai Volcano National Park: The only place flowing lava can be witnessed in the Islands. http://www.kauai.com/kauai-geography

CHAPTER NINE

39. S&P 500 Crash, October 2007 to March 2009: Protecting Your Portfolio http://news.morningstar.com/articlenet/article.aspx?id=309304
40. NASDAQ Crash, March 2000 to October 2002, A Guide: http://www. wisestockbuyer.com/a-guide-to-the-2001-tech-crash/

CHAPTER TEN

41. SS Ville du Havre: On November 22, 1873 the passenger ship Ville du Havre was rammed by the iron clipper Loch Earn in the North Atlantic about 680 miles northwest of the Azores. http://www.maritimequest.com/daily_event_archive/2007/pages/nov/22_ss_ville_du_havre.htm
42. Excerpt from "When Peace Like A River" Author: Horatio Gates Spafford. https://hymnary.org/text/when_peace_like_a_river_attendeth_my_way

CHAPTER ELEVEN

43. Permian Basin: Large sedimentary basin in western Texas and southeastern New Mexico, U.S., noted for its rich petroleum, natural gas, and potassium deposits. https://www.britannica.com/place/Permian-Basin
44. The Petroleum Building: (formerly known as the Hogan Building) Is a high-rise in downtown Midland, TX. The building was built in 1928 and consists of 12 floors and has a neo-gothic style architecture to it. The building stands at 137 feet but with its spires reaches a height of 151 feet. The Hogan building is a registered, Texas historical landmark. The tower is named for lawyer and oil entrepreneur Thomas Stephen Hogan. Additional Photographs at: https://texashistory.unt.edu/search/?q=Petroleum+Building+in+Midland&t=fulltext&sort=
45. Friday Night Lights, 25th Anniversary Edition: A Town, a Team and a Dream—August 11, 2015 by H.G. Bissinger
46. The Midland Rock Hounds: Are a minor league baseball team based in Midland, Texas. The team, which plays in the Texas League, is the Double-A affiliate of the Oakland Athletics major league club. https://en.wikipedia.org/wiki/Midland_RockHounds
47. Joseph Chris Carter (born March 7, 1960): Is an American former professional baseball player. He played in Major League Baseball (MLB) as an outfielder and first baseman for the Chicago Cubs, Cleveland Indians, San Diego Padres, Toronto Blue Jays, Baltimore Orioles, and San Francisco Giants. Carter is best known for hitting a walk-off home run to win the 1993 World Series for the Toronto Blue Jays. https://en.wikipedia.org/wiki/Joe_Carter
48. James Patrick Edmonds (born June 27, 1970): Is an American former center fielder in Major League Baseball and a current broadcaster for Fox Sports Midwest. https://en.wikipedia.org/wiki/Jim_Edmonds

49. Barry William Zito (born May 13, 1978): Is an American former professional baseball pitcher and musician. He played 15 seasons in Major League Baseball (MLB) for the Oakland Athletics and San Francisco Giants. https://en.wikipedia.org/wiki/Barry_Zito

50. Shawon Donnell Dunston (born March 21, 1963): Is an American retired professional baseball player. A shortstop, Dunston played in Major League Baseball (MLB) from 1985 through 2002. https://en.wikipedia.org/wiki/Shawon_Dunston

51. Sanford Koufax Born December 30, 1935: Hall of Fame 1972 https://baseballhall.org/hof/koufax-sandy

52. Lynn Nolan Ryan Jr. was born January 31, 1947: In Refugio, Texas. He was the youngest of six children of Lynn Nolan Ryan Sr. and Martha Ryan. Ryan grew up in Alvin, Texas, where his father worked for an oil company and delivered papers for the *Houston Post*. Ryan credits his father for instilling in him the value of a strong work ethic. In second grade, Ryan began helping his father on his paper routes. http://www.notablebiographies.com/Ro-Sc/Ryan-Nolan.html#ixzz516uESUtK

53. The Wagner Noël Performing Arts Center: Was the vision of several community and civic leaders in Midland and Odessa. In 2006 that vision was realized when Texas Legislation was authorized for the construction of a performing arts facility and music department for The University of Texas of the Permian Basin. http://wagnernoel.com/about/

54. Seven Age Related Tips; 55 to $70^{1/2}$, from the Balance.com, US News and World Report, IRS and Social Security: https://www.thebalance.com/your-retirement-plan-timeline-2388844 https://money.usnews.com/money/retirement/articles/2012/02/21/10-important-ages-for-retirement-planning Publication 554: https://www.irs.gov/publications/p554
Social Security Matters: https://blog.ssa.gov/the-best-age-for-you-to-retire/Retirement Planner: The Difference Between Retirement Age & Stop Work Age: https://www.ssa.gov/planners/retire/stopwork.html

CHAPTER TWELVE

55. Sloan Field Midland International Airport: Was originally Sloan Field, a small airport started in 1927 by Samuel Addison Sloan. http://www.flymaf.com/137/Army-Airfield

56. The Commemorative Air Force: Or CAF Website is where the CAF showcases our Warbirds, our fleet of historic World War II Aircraft. https://www.commemorativeairforce.org/

57. Reese Air Force Base: Hearing the Winds of War in 1941, the City of Lubbock offered 2,000 acres to the War Department to build an airfield. http://www.insyteinc.com/reese.htm

58. Fort Bragg: It is the home of the Army's XVIII Airborne Corps and is the headquarters of the United States Army Special Operations Command, which

oversees the U.S. Army 1st Special Forces Command (Airborne) (Provisional) and 75th Ranger Regiment. https://en.wikipedia.org/wiki/Fort_Bragg

59. The Tomb of the Unknown Soldier: At Arlington National Cemetery stands atop a hill overlooking Washington, D.C. On March 4, 1921, Congress approved the burial of an unidentified American soldier from World War I in the plaza of the new Memorial Amphitheater. http://www.arlingtoncemetery.mil/explore/tomb-of-the-unknown-soldier

60. IRS Contributions Limits to Your IRA, Roth IRA: Retirement Topics—IRA Contribution Limits https://www.irs.gov/retirement-plans/plan-participant-employee/retirement-topics-ira-contribution-limits Retirement Plans FAQs on Designated Roth Accounts https://www.irs.gov/retirement-plans/retirement-plans-faqs-on-designated-roth-accounts

CHAPTER THIRTEEN

61. William Tecumseh Sherman: American Civil War general and a major architect of modern warfare. https://www.britannica.com/biography/William-Tecumseh-Sherman

62. Figures on U.S. Debt: From the National Debt Clock $20.63 February 2018 Trillion. http://www.usdebtclock.org/

63. Gross Domestic Product: (Everything we make and build in the U.S.) As of February 2018 it is at $19.79 Trillion.

64. GDP Ratio: As of February 2018 the GDP ratio is at 104.20%. http://www.usdebtclock.org/

65. U.S. Economy Grows: As of February 26, 2016 It's been a decade since we had 3 percent growth. The longest consecutive stretch of years in which the United State saw real GDP grow by 3.0 percent or better was the seven year period from 1983-1989, during the presidency of Ronald Reagan. https://www.cnsnews.com/news/article/terence-p-jeffrey/us-has-record-10th-straight-year-without-3-growth-gdp

66. Inflating money: There is over four trillion dollars to pay back. Four Stories of Quantitative Easing https://files.stlouisfed.org/files/htdocs/publications/review/13/01/Fawley.pdf

67. Gonzales, TX: Birthplace of Texas Independence and home of the Come & Take It Cannon! http://gonzalestexas.com/historic-walking-tour/

68. Molon Labe: The history, meaning and the pronunciation of two very powerful words spoken by King Leonidas that have lived for two and a half Millennia. https://en.wikipedia.org/wiki/Molon_labe

69. Civil Wars Deaths Toll—Science: New Estimate Raises Civil War Death Toll. https://opinionator.blogs.nytimes.com/2011/09/20/recounting-the-dead/#more-105317

70. Medicare, Medicaid & Social Security Future Commitments: http://www.milkeninstitute.org/events/conferences/global-conference/2008/panel-detail/1193

71. Average Social Security Benefit Yearly: https://www.cbpp.org/research/social-security/social-security-benefits-are-modest

CHAPTER FOURTEEN

72. Thomas Fuller: British scholar, preacher, and one of the most witty and prolific authors of the 17th century. Fuller was educated at Queens' College, Cambridge. https://www.britannica.com/biography/Thomas-Fuller
73. Giving USA Year 2016 Annual Report: https://nonprofitquarterly.org/2017/06/13/giving-usas-numbers-2016-reflect-historic-opportunity/
74. The Bynum School: In Midland, TX is a private, non-profit, year-round special needs school for ages 3 to adult. http://www.bynumschool.org/
75. The Scranton Academy for Financial Education: Is dedicated to providing no-cost financial education as a public service. https://midamerican.fixedincomecounsel.com/s-a-f-e/
76. Permian Basin Honor Flight Committee, Permian Basin Area Foundation: http://www.pbaf.org/2017/06/permian-basin-area-foundation-awards-1-5-million-in-spring-grant-cycle/
77. Peter Lynch Born: Newton, Massachusetts, January 19, 1944. https://en.wikipedia.org/wiki/Peter_Lynch
78. GuideStar's gathers and distributes nonprofit information to help people make better decisions. https://learn.guidestar.org/about-us/
79. Charity Navigator: Is an American independent charity watchdog organization that evaluates charitable organizations in the United States. https://www.directrelief.org/2017/01/ten-of-the-best-charities-direct-relief-tops-charity-navigators-list/
80. Social Security Retirement: Ready To Retire https://www.ssa.gov/retireonline

CHAPTER FIFTEEN

81. DJIA: Time to Break Even October 10th 2007 to March 6th 2013 Source: Yahoo Finance Historical Data https://finance.yahoo.com/quote/%5EDJI/history?ltr=1
82. DJIA: Plummets 54% According to Houston Chronicle: http://blog.chron.com/txpotomac/2012/09/high-points-and-low-points-of-the-obama-presidency/
83. U.S. Energy Information Administration - Petroleum, Liquids: https://www.eia.gov/dnav/pet/hist/LeafHandler.ashx?n=-PET&s=F000000__3&f=M

CHAPTER SIXTEEN

84. Current Savings Rate—Best High-Yield Online Accounts: https://www.nerdwallet.com/blog/banking/best-high-yield-online-savings-accounts/

85. Percentage of Americans with Money in U.S. Stock Market: https://www.bloomberg.com/view/articles/2018-02-06/the-stock-market-is-a-lot-like-bitcoin

86. Major Financial Scandals—Banks Have Paid $321 Billion: http://fortune.com/2017/03/03/bank-fines-2008-financial-crisis/

87. NASDAQ Drops 9-2002, What Causes a Stock Market Crash: http://www.telegraph.co.uk/business/2017/07/14/causes-stock-market-crash-headed-another/

88. Case-Shiller U.S. National Home Price Index: FRED Economic Data, Federal Reserve Bank Of St. Louis, Economic Research, https://fred.stlouisfed.org/series/CSUSHPINSA

89. The Federal Reserve System: Is the central bank of the United States. It performs five general functions to promote the effective operation of the U.S. economy and, more generally, the public interest. https://www.federalreserve.gov/aboutthefed.htm

90. Legerdemain Definition: Sleight of hand; a display of skill or adroitness. https://www.merriamwebster.com/dictionary/legerdemain

CHAPTER SEVENTEEN

91. Abraham Lincoln: "The problem with internet quotes is that you can't always depend on their accuracy": You are likely to have a friend or frenemy post one to you after you post something they don't believe to be true or accurate. https://www.thoughtco.com/the-problem-with-quotes-on-the-internet-3970560

92. Leonardo da Vinci: Was born on 15 April 1452 in Anchiano, near Vinci, Republic of Florence. https://www.britannica.com/biography/Leonardo-da-Vinci

CHAPTER NINETEEN

93. Eeyores: The gloomy donkey of the Winnie the Pooh book series, by extension a pessimistic or depressed person. http://www.dictionary.com/browse/eeyore

94. KALYDECO: Is a prescription medicine used for the treatment of cystic fibrosis (CF) https://www.kalydeco.com/

95. Advisors' Academy: Was founded in 2007 by David J. Scranton with a vision to recruit other highly successful, motivated advisors and teach them how to achieve even higher levels of success—while always putting the interests of their clients first! https://advisorsacademy.com/#about

DEE'S DIRECTIVES

CHARTS

CHAPTER 6

Page 65
Chart A
Dow Jones Industrial Average October 2007 to March 2009
Source: Yahoo Finance DJIA Historical Data
https://finance.yahoo.com/quote/%5EDJI/history?ltr=1

CHAPTER 7

Page 79
Chart B
Dow Jones Industrial Average Daily Closing 1966 To 1988
Source: https://www.measuringworth.com/datasets/DJA/result.php
Citation: Samuel H. Williamson, 'Daily Closing Value of the Dow Jones
Average, 1885 to Present,' MeasuringWorth, 2018.

CHAPTER 9

Page 106
Chart C
Standard and Poor's 500 October 2007 to March 2009
Source: Yahoo Finance S&P 500 Historical Data
https://finance.yahoo.com/quote/%5EGSPC/history?ltr=1

CHAPTER 16

Page 185
Chart D
Investments: Risk Tolerance—Conservative, Moderate, Aggressive
MLPs Master Limited Partnerships—Source: https://www.forbes.com/sites/
advisor/2014/09/30/what-you-need-to-know-about-mlps-and-investing-in-
energy/#4317c6717db7
BDCs Business Development Company—Source: https://en.wikipedia.org/
wiki/Business_Development_Company
Chart: Courtesy—Clear Choice Graphics

INDEX

ABOUT THE AUTHOR

DEE K. CARTER is the founder of The Carter Financial Group. The firm is still active and strong in Midland with over 800 clients. He became associated with The Advisors' Academy in 2011 and serves on the Advisory Board of that marketing firm. He is also an Investment Advisor Representative with Sound Income Strategies, an SEC approved brokerage firm with headquarters in Fort Lauderdale, Florida.

Dee has been active in many different programs in the Midland area including the Northwest YMCA (board member), The Midland Association for Retarded Citizens (board member), the Southwest Basketball Officials Association (board member and Secretary for 13 years), The Midland Odessa Symphony and Chorale (board member and Chorale member), The Midland Downtown Lions' Club (Foundation board member) and served as a basketball official (high school and college) for 28 years. He has been a member of The National Association of Insurance and Financial Advisors-Texas since 1976, serving as the State President of that organization in 2000-01. He received the Lifetime Achievement Award from NAIFA-Texas in 2012 and was recognized as Lifetime Member of the Southwest Officials Association in 2002. He was also a nationally recognized Elvis Tribute Artist for 15 years, and was a finalist for the Elvis Impersonator of the Year in 2004. Dee has a weekly radio program each Monday morning at 8:00 on KWEL 1070 AM and 107.1 FM, where he discusses retirement planning. He has been recognized as a leader for American Equity Investment Life Insurance Company appearing on their Agents' Forum program in March of 2018.

Dee is married to the former Susan Hanes (June 22, 1976). Their family includes: Erin and Mandee and from a previous marriage:

Randa Lang of Lubbock, Texas and Devyn Carter of Atlanta, Georgia. Dee and Susan have three grandchildren: Ashley and Brady Lang and Lily Carter. He and his daughter, Mandee, are partners in The Carter Financial Group in Midland, Texas.